A PARTY BOOK TO USE YEAR AFTER YEAR

"It worked for me" . . . Parents share their best ideas. One mother invited a pet store owner who brought a small menagerie. . . . "Her fee was free because I bought Betas and mini–fish bowls from her store as party favors."

Invitations . . . Make your own theme invitations. Don't miss the darling Garden Party ideas!

Activities . . . Fun games and projects that will bolster every child's self-esteem. The Fossil Stepping Stone from the "Dinosaur's Rule" is a sure winner.

Party Starters . . . Get partygoers in the mood the moment they step through the door with crowns, hats, or even a custom-made "license plate." See the Road Race party for directions.

Decorations . . . Set the scene—with a minimum of mess—for pennies. Boys will love the "Construction Site" party set off with black-and-yellow caution tape and plastic hard hats.

Food . . . Imaginative, appetizing treats: Don't miss the "Campsite Cake" that captures the delicious flavors of S'mores, or the Name Your Sundae buffet to top off your Ice Cream Social.

Party Favors . . . A keepsake that may become a child's favorite treasure, such as the "magic gadget" from the Alakazam party's amazing afternoon of wonder and wishes.

THE PARENTS PARTY BOOK

W9-CJH-210

**DON'T MISS THESE
OTHER PARENTS PICKS BOOKS**

THE PARENTS ANSWER BOOK

YOUR ONE-YEAR-OLD

YOUR TWO-YEAR-OLD

THE ACTIVITY BOOK

IT WORKED FOR ME!

**AVAILABLE FROM
ST. MARTIN'S PAPERBACKS**

The Parents Party Book

Fun and Fabulous Theme Birthday Parties for Children 2 to 8 Years Old

By the editors of *Parents* magazine and Eleanor Levie

St. Martin's Paperbacks

THE PARENTS PARTY BOOK

Copyright © 1999 by Roundtable Press, Inc. and G+J USA Publishing.

Cover photograph © Strauss/Curtis/CORBIS

Library of Congress Catalog Card Number: 99-13235

ISBN: 0-312-98872-9

Printed in the United States of America

St. Martin's Paperbacks edition / April 2004

St. Martin's Paperbacks are published by St. Martin's Press, 175 Fifth Avenue, New York, NY 10010.

10 9 8 7 6 5 4 3 2 1

ACKNOWLEDGMENTS

I am grateful to the following people who have shared their wonderfully creative ideas with me for this book: Carl Harrington, Sam Harrington, Sammie Moshenberg, Roberta Yakovich, Teresa Hanas, Sue Wells, Nancy Armo, Patricia Harste, Ogden Kruger, Jude Muse, Marc Silver, and Aaron Levie.

—Eleanor Levie

CONTENTS

FOREWORD

For children, a special party is often the best reason to have a birthday. The fact that they're commemorating the miraculous day on which they were born, that they're actually turning a whole year older, is merely icing on their already well-decorated cake!

As parents, we also love to celebrate our children's birthdays. However, planning the party often looms so large in our minds that we lose sight of the purpose of the event—in a word, FUN. This book puts the fun back into children's parties by taking the guesswork out. We've created a theme for each of the 36 parties here, and then given you a foolproof list of easy-to-make invitations, decorations, activities, food, crafts, and even favors. We've included start-to-finish game plans, timetables, gift suggestions, menus, and perhaps most important of all, tips from other parents.

Each page is so chock-full of ideas that your hardest decision is going to be what to do this year . . . and what to save for next. My advice: Let your child be the judge. This is his, or her, day. There are teddy bear picnics and carnivals, backwards birthdays, luaus, tea parties, and Hollywood bashes. In fact, I bet there are a few parties you wouldn't mind throwing for yourself—which only proves that you're never too old to have a happy birthday.

Sally Lee
Editor-in-Chief

Introduction

Each party in this book revolves around a theme that is sure to delight children from 2 through 8 years old. You can use the parties as you find them or mix and match the elements. Helpful party-giving guides, described here, will help you plan a celebration in which you, your child, and all the guests will enjoy a wonderful, stress-free time. A brief introduction to each party indicates the ages that will most enjoy the activities.

Invitation

In each party description, you'll find ideas for clever invitations that let guests anticipate the special events of the celebration to come. If your child enjoys arts and crafts, he or she can probably give you a hand with making these.

Decorations

Decorations set the stage and keep everyone in a party mood. Ideas given in this section range from quick and easy to ambitious. Use as many as your time and budget permit.

Party Starters

These ice breakers involve the kids in a reassuring, creative, and nonthreatening way as they arrive. Once everyone has arrived, move to the most significant activity.

Activities

The games and challenges in this book are usually a chance for kids to get physical, let off steam, and burn up energy. Be concise when you present game rules, because you won't have the kids' attention for long; if you can, arrange for another adult or a teenager to help supervise. When a game requires that children take turns, such as in a relay race, follow it up with a physical challenge everyone can do simultaneously. If you sense that a game is too challenging or not challenging enough, cut it short and move on to something else. The emergency games on page 54 are good to keep in the back of your head—or on a slip of paper in a pocket. But don't feel you have to produce all the activities suggested for a party, if the array seems too generous for the time available or the age of your child. Pick the ones you find most appropriate and appealing.

A short cleanup after active play is essential when food is going to be served. If time or facilities are limited, portable wipes can do the trick. Also before refreshments, help kids catch their breath, settle down, and get calm, perhaps with a story or song.

Food

Allow plenty of time for eating, including the ritual of singing "Happy Birthday" and blowing out the candles. If the dessert suggested for the party you've chosen is individual cupcakes or cookies rather than a cake, be sure to arrange them with candles on a serving platter so that your child will enjoy the full ceremony.

Story Time

Children love being read to and looking at pictures. This gently paced activity will inspire the kids with an aspect of your theme and give them some food for thought. Schedule story time after intense physical activity to allow the kids to calm down. The books listed here are just suggestions; many other excellent titles exist. Your local librarian or bookstore clerk could help you find several.

Party Favor

Have some sort of favor or small gift for each guest to take home. This is a nice way to say thank you and lets the guest remember the party. One word of caution: Avoid customized goody bags, which can lead to disappointment for some of your child's friends.

Bear's Best Birthday

Bear cubs (a.k.a. your toddler and his friends) will be charmed by this "make-believe" fête. When young guests bring a favorite teddy bear or other "lovey" along, they feel secure, comfortable, and ready for a romp. So prepare to suspend your disbelief and enjoy the festivities. If you become Mama Bear or Papa Bear, you'll be rewarded with broad smiles and bear hugs all around.

Invitation
Photocopy a coloring-book teddy bear and write the party particulars on it. Ask each guest to bring a favorite teddy bear—or any beloved stuffed animal.

Decorations
- Spread out a checkered tablecloth and picnic basket on the ground—or, for an indoor party, on the floor.
- Suggest a backwoods environment with container plants or oversized foam-board cutouts of berry bushes and trees (make one with a beehive).
- Turn a big appliance box, a table covered with a floor-length cloth, or a pup tent into a "cave" for kids to crawl into.
- Set out plates of teddy bear graham cracker cookies for anytime snacking.

Party Starters

Bear's New Duds

Shy kids will get their bear-ings by focusing attention on the stuffed animals they brought from home. Put out a collection of felt and straw doll hats from the craft store, plus assorted ribbons, feathers, and some quick-setting glue. Let kids find and embellish a hat for their plush toy, or at least tie a new ribbon around its neck or middle (have an older child nearby to help).

Join the Cub Club

Turn each arrival into a little bear club: Before the party, cut out small circles or "ears" from tan or brown craft foam. Pinch the bottoms so the ears cup slightly, then hot-glue them to headbands or baseball caps.

Activities

Follow That Bear

Bear cub kids follow you, their grizzly bear leader, through the woods of your imagination. Narrate your adventures as you pretend to climb up a tree, nose around for honey, see some bees and run away, amble over to a stream, take a drink, catch fish, search for berries, and lumber toward slumber in a cave. Any makeshift props will add to the fun.

Awards Ceremony

Line up the stuffed guests and award a ribbon to each, bearing testimony to their being the most huggable, the fuzziest, the noisiest, the softest, or whatever comes to mind.

Food

Ice Cream Bears

Place a scoop of ice cream in a shallow bowl and add round wafer cookie ears. With red decorator icing in a tube, draw a smile, nose, and eyes. Use chocolate ice cream for brown bears, vanilla ice cream for polar bears and pandas. A squeeze of chocolate sauce around the eyes creates the panda's face.

Story Time

   Little Bear by Else Holmelund Minarik (Harper-
      Collins). Four little stories include a trip to the
      moon and having a birthday party.
   Corduroy by Don Freeman (Viking Press). A toy
      bear in a department store wants a home and a
      friend.
   The Teddy Bears' Picnic by Jimmy Kennedy
      (Green Tiger Press). Based on the lyrics of a
      song, this story shows teddy bears cavorting in
      the woods, then heading home.
   Jesse Bear, What Will You Wear? by Nancy White
      Carlstrom (Macmillan). Lilting rhymes tell what
      Jesse Bear will wear—including a bear hug.

Party Favor

In addition to the hat, let each child choose a small book to take home and read over and over with Mama Bear or Papa Bear.

INVOLVING THE BIRTHDAY CHILD

Choose the Theme

If your child is 4 years old or over, the most important way to involve him in planning his birthday party is to let him help choose a theme. Limiting yourselves to a single theme helps to focus most aspects of the party, makes them easier to plan, and makes the party more fun. Start about a month beforehand by looking at this book together, browsing at party stores, and talking about previous parties your child has enjoyed. Ask your child for ideas, but be prepared with some suggestions. Younger children may be confused if you offer more than three choices. Discuss how the party might help your child live out his or her fantasy—being royalty for a day, perhaps, or going on an underwater adventure—and choose one of the included parties (or develop one of your own) that will let the dream come true. Make sure, though, that the theme is in the realm of possibility for you and your budget. If you can't manage a real nature adventure, work out a compromise, like the Love-A-Bug! party (page 24) or the Happy Trails "pretend" campout (page 194). You can always tweak any favorite game, recipe, or craft to make it relate to the chosen theme in some small way.

INVOLVING THE BIRTHDAY CHILD

Use Your Child's Skills

Let your child help with making invitations or decorations—or even some of the food. Depending on his age, he may be able to color in or even draw images for the invitation, make crêpe paper flowers, hang streamers, or slice fruit.

Similarly, let your child help design stationery for thank-you notes a day or two after the party. Photocopy a form letter or compose one on your home computer, but encourage your child to help you personalize each one. If the child is too young to write, have her make a handprint or dictate the letter. She might simply fill in the blanks: "Thank you for the _____. I like it because _____." Rubber stamps are great for letting kids decorate multiple invitations and thank-you notes.

Use Your Child's Ideas

Discuss the possibilities for activities, craft projects, and foods. Most girls and boys will have definite ideas about every specific detail. After you've decided what you'll do and have at the party, drop the subject for a few days. However, go over the agenda for the party the day before to refresh your child's memory—and yours!

Block Party

Host a gentle blockbuster to mark a little one's big day. For a child turning 2 or 3 years old, this sweet celebration might be a glorified play group get-together. Invite just a couple of children of a similar age and their parents. Rather than blocking off time for certain activities, stay flexible. Expect parallel play and be receptive to individual interests. Let parents assist their own children and respond to their joy or flagging attention.

Invitation

Send a ready-to-assemble "baby block": Purchase collapsible white gift boxes, each approximately 4 cubic inches. Write "Come to a Block Party" and all the necessary information on one side. Write A, B, C on the three other sides and stencil two simple graphics, such as a duck and teddy bear, on the remaining sides. The receiver can form it into a block shape. (Decorate some additional boxes without the party data to use for serving snacks.)

Decorations

- Find a cubic box large enough for small fry to crawl inside; remove the top, then cut a big window in one side and a door flap in another side. Paint the box or cover the exterior with self-adhesive vinyl. Paint or glue on letters and animal shapes.

- Scatter wood and plastic building blocks all around, available for play at any time.
- Spell out HAPPY BIRTHDAY or your child's name in alphabet blocks.
- Set out square crackers, such as saltines, in the extra decorated invitation boxes. Arrange juice boxes in a pyramid.

Party Starters

Blockhouse
Let toddlers climb into the giant block. Play peekaboo with the window or door flap, and show them how to pop up and down like a jack-in-the-box. Sing "Pop Goes the Weasel."

Activities

Block Printing
Beforehand: Make at least one sponge stamp for each child to use. For each, cut a household sponge into a square and glue it to a similarly sized piece of wood. Glue on an empty spool (or a similar piece of wood) for a handle.

At the party: Squeeze finger paints in two or three colors into disposable aluminum pie pans. Give each child a large piece of freezer paper; place the paper, matte side up, on the table. Help each child press a stamp into some paint, then onto the paper, making a random pattern of squares.

Excitement Is Building

Encourage a child or two to stack blocks as high as possible before they come tumbling down. Then laugh and build the tower up again!

Food

Baby Blocks

Buy or make petits-fours—tiny cubes of layer cake iced on all sides. Use decorator icing in tubes to pipe the number of the birthday on each cake. Arrange the cakes on a platter around a number candle. If you wish, serve with cubes of sherbet (spooned into ice cube trays before the party).

Story Time

Spot Looks at Shapes by Eric Hill (Putnam). An appealing cardboard book toddlers can hold and touch.

Shapes, Shapes, Shapes by Tana Hoben (William Morrow). Photographs of familiar things.

Party Favor

Give each little guest a soft block or other small, clutchable toy. Send the parents home with a photo cube or square picture mat for displaying snapshots of their own chip-off-the-old-block children. If you have an instant camera, you might want to include a picture taken during the party for each parent.

KEEP IT SAFE

The party should be fun for everyone. Select or set up the location, plan the activities, and prepare the food with safety in mind.

- Have enough adults on hand to help you lead the activities, supervise the children, and serve the food. Even if you can do it all, you can't be everywhere at once—and if something should go awry, you'll need backup.

- If you'll be going to a location other than your home, be sure to visit it first. Do this even if it's your local playground; you should think through the plan of action on site.

- Have a first-aid kit handy. Colorful bandages will keep small booboos from spoiling the fun. Be sure you know the emergency phone numbers for your location—just in case.

- Remember that certain foods can present a choking hazard for small children. Toddler-safe foods are soft, bite-size, and finger-friendly. Even if your child is older, be sure not to serve the following to any guests under 5:

     Hard candies
     Popcorn

KEEP IT SAFE

> Raw vegetables or fruits cut into coin
> shapes
> Grapes and cherries, unless sliced
> lengthwise in half
> Apples, unless sliced
> Nuts
> Hot-dog pieces

- Be savvy about allergies. Strawberries are a common allergen, with hives being the primary reaction. Peanuts are a less common problem, but the reaction to them is more dangerous. Older children will know if they are allergic to peanuts, but young ones may not. Also, peanuts lurk in some prepared foods, such as the hard candy shell on small chocolates. Leave strawberries, peanuts and peanut products, and candy-coated chocolates off the menu.

- If you are aware of an outbreak of lice in your child's school, refrain from including dress-up activities that feature hats or wigs.

Rainbows

Rain or shine, this party's fine! If your child is turning 2 or 3, brighten her big day with good friends, pretty hues, and foods with plenty of eye appeal.

Invitation

Begin with sheets of watercolor paper cut to fit inside a legal envelope. Sponge water over the paper and have your child stroke on watercolor paints. The paints will bleed into one another like a true rainbow. When dry, write the details on top with a black marker.

Decorations

- Tie Mylar balloons in lots of colors at the mailbox, indicating the party site.
- Cut out one or more big poster-board clouds. Using spray adhesive, cover them with puffs of white polyester stuffing and then tape on colorful crêpe paper streamers. Affix the clouds to the wall or ceiling with double-stick foam tape. If you have a chandelier over the party table, festoon it with polyester stuffing and more streamers.
- Dangle large plastic prisms from light fixtures for iridescent plays of light and subtle dazzle.
- Set out stacking rings, shape sorters, beach balls, and other multicolored, toddler-safe toys.

Party Starters

Rainbow Necklaces

Put out a big bowl of colored loop cereal and give each child a licorice or red candy lace for stringing on the o-shapes. When the job is done—which may total 3 or 20 pieces of cereal—knot together the lace ends.

Paint Me a Rainbow

Spread plastic over a worktable. Set out paper and fat, washable markers. Ask the kids to draw rainbows—or simply to add lots of colors to their papers. After they're done, they can spray water from a plant mister onto their paper and watch the colors run. Demonstrate by making a rainbow yourself to reassure anyone who seems unhappy about having his work altered.

Activities

Bubblemania

Blow bubbles, using a purchased jar of soapy water plus wand. Kids love running after bubbles to try to burst them, and trying to blow bubbles themselves (you could hold the just-dipped wand). Consider borrowing or purchasing a huge wand, which works best when dipped into a kiddie pool filled with water, dishwashing detergent, and some corn syrup (to keep the bubbles from popping too soon). Mega-bubbles! It's just possible that a bubble will last long enough for everyone to notice the rainbow iridescence.

Wet and Wonderful

On a sunny summer day, set out the sprinkler and you might see a real rainbow. A perforated-hose sprinkler makes rainbows, as does the mist setting on a hose nozzle. Let bathing-suited kids run through it.

Chance of Rain

Beforehand: Cut out big teardrop shapes from white self-adhesive vinyl, unpeel the paper backing and stick them to a rain slicker or windbreaker so that they're easy to access.

To play: Wear this gear in your role as meteorologist; carry an umbrella, too. Choose one child to be a raindrop, with a sticker applied to his chest, and station him a short distance away from you. Have kids stroll around as you deliver a sunny weather report: "The weather's fine!" All of a sudden, open your umbrella and say, "It's raining!" At that point, the designated raindrop tries to tag the other players. Anyone who is caught becomes a raindrop too, and helps catch the others. Continue to close and open your umbrella until everyone gets turned into a raindrop. Reward the players with a gold notary sticker, to represent the sun. Then explain that sun plus raindrops gives us rainbows, and issue everyone a rainbow sticker to wear as well.

Food

Rainbow Fruit Salad

Make rows of fresh, sliced favorites: watermelon, oranges, red and green apples, kiwi, blueberries, pears—whatever is popular with your guests.

Rainbow Desserts

Dip just-iced mini cupcakes into a bowl of rainbow sprinkles to coat the tops. Or, use decorator gels in tubes to squeeze arches of four or five colors over cupcakes with vanilla frosting. Scoop rainbow sherbet into 3-ounce paper or plastic cups—no spoons necessary.

Story Time

Sun, Snow, Stars, Sky by Catherine and Laurence Anholt (Viking Press). Charming watercolor pictures invite young children to think and talk about the weather.

A Rainbow of My Own by Don Freeman (Viking Press). A boy imagines he has his own rainbow to play with.

A Rainbow at Night by Bruce Hucko (Chronicle Books). Tales of Navajo children.

Party Favor

In a clear cellophane bag, drop a jar of bubble juice, a mini prism-viewer, and a package of colorful fruit cereal. Tie it with several strands of curling ribbon in different colors. Invite kids to transfer their necklace, raindrop, and notary stickers to this bag.

"IT WORKED FOR ME"

"We had my daughter's birthday party in a park on a hot day. To keep everyone cool, I brought spray bottles (the kind you mist plants with) filled with water. The kids had a great time getting wet and cooling off. Make just one rule: Stop means stop—whether said by a child or an adult."

Puppy Party

Kids will howl with glee as they play pup for a day. Here's a silly party designed especially for frisky toddlers and preschoolers. Paw-print decor, dog-bone cookies, and guess what for goody bags—what more could a young pooch want? So, invite your guests to bring a favorite plush puppy or bean-bag toy along; stage a little dog show and give ribbons to everyone's plush pet.

Invitation

Cut dog-bone shapes from brown grocery bags (you can trace around a dog-bone cookie cutter or a large dog biscuit) and fill in all the information about your bowzer bash.

Decorations

- Sponge-paint paw prints all over a solid-color plastic tablecloth: Cut one big and four small circles from a household sponge. Glue them to a block of wood, arranging the small circles in an arc above the big one. When the glue is dry, moisten the sponges. Dip them in a plate of acrylic paint and stamp the design all over the tablecloth. If your kids are 4 or over, let them help or stamp a welcome mat or birthday sign using the same paw print.
- Make a big cardboard box doghouse with one doorway in front and another in back so that kids

can crawl through. Write the birthday child's name over the doorways.

- Serve snacks in plastic dog bowls on the table—a treat for toddlers who are being taught not to eat from the pets' dishes on the floor.

Party Starters

Put on a Puppy Face

Beforehand: Tie or sew lengths of soft black elastic to fit comfortably around your child's head. Cut floppy ears from felt and glue a pair onto each elastic band. Make some bands large enough for adults or older children too.

At the party: As each guest arrives, place the ears around his head. Then use face paint to blacken or rouge the ball of his nose, and to draw some spots and whiskers.

Dog Tags

These ID tags are made using shrink-art plastic sheets from the craft store, which, when baked, shrink about 60 percent. Each child can wear one on a ribbon around her waist at the party, or tie it around her plush pet's neck.

Beforehand: Cut the shrink-art sheets widthwise in thirds, then cut them into dog-bone shapes as you did the invitations. Use a hole punch to make a hole at the center of one short end of each.

At the party: Working with each child and using permanent marker, write the desired name and perhaps a telephone number on a bone shape.

Let kids crayon over the surface. Bake the tags on a cookie sheet in a preheated 275°F oven for about three minutes, or until the shrink-art plastic has shrunk, uncurled, and again lies flat. Remove with a spatula, let cool for a minute or two, and slip a jump ring or narrow ribbon through the hole.

PARENTS ALERT

Kids love to watch the shrinking process through the oven window. If your oven has no window, crack the door open after two minutes so they can see the change. Don't let the kids handle the oven or the hot cookie sheet.

Activities

Dog Tricks
Kids have (p)oodles of fun and learn canine commands, too. See who can bark the loudest when asked to "Speak!" Let them roll over, shake hands with their front "paw," stay, and heel. Reward each good dog with a dog-bone cookie (see p. 22).

In the Doghouse
Play music while kids crawl through the cardboard-box doghouse. "How Much Is That Doggie in the Window?" would be a terrier-ific choice! When the music stops, whoever is in the doghouse wins a treat.

Doggone It
In this hide-and-seek variation, one child sits in the makeshift doghouse while everyone else hides himself or his stuffed animal.

Doggie, Doggie
In this classic game, one person—start with a clever canine impersonator—leaves the room, and someone takes a dog bone into her possession. When the first player returns, everyone says, "Doggie, Doggie, somebody has your bone!" Doggie looks around for someone suspicious, and says, "Is it you?" When the bone burglar is collared, he becomes Doggie for the next round.

Food

Dog-bone Cookies
Use a dog-bone-shaped cookie cutter with any rolled-out cookie dough.

Pupcakes
Cut floppy ears from pressed fruit snack food and sink them into the sides of a cupcake iced with any color. Add small candy eyes, a peanut-butter cup muzzle, and a gumdrop nose. Create a mouth, a shaggy mane, and perhaps a spot with decorator gel in a tube.

Story Time
Harry, the Dirty Dog by Gene Zion (Harpercrest).
   Will anyone recognize the beloved family pooch?

Officer Buckle and Gloria by Peggy Rathmann
(Putnam). A police dog who can really bow-
wow a crowd.

Clifford the Big Red Dog by Norman Bridwell
(Scholastic). An absolutely huge and lovable
dog, loved by his owner and every reader.

For the littlest children, any of the Spot books by Eric
Hill (Putnam). These are cardboard books with simple
plots.

Party Favor

A doggie bag, natch! Use white or brown lunch bags and
construction paper. From the construction paper, cut out
shapes for eyes, muzzle, and floppy ears. Use a black
marker to add a big spot behind one eye, pupils to each
eye, a nose, smile, and dots to the muzzle. Glue the eyes
and muzzle to the front of the bag, and ears to the sides,
starting 5" down from the top. For a long-haired, mop-
top look, cut a 2"-wide fringe along the top 5" through
all layers; open the bag and fold down the fringe over
each side.

For quick-and-easy doggie bags, just stamp lunch
bags with paw prints.

Fill the doggie bag with dog stickers and, of course, a
few dog-bone cookies; slip in the dog tag if the child is
not wearing it.

Love-A-Bug!

"Buzz" on—this party provides more than just a mite of fun. Smaller tykes will make a beeline for this happy bee-day party. Churn up the challenge for older children by featuring a walk in the woods with a nature center guide, or perhaps an "ant" or uncle who can help identify various insects.

Invitation

Make a ladybug whose wings fan out to reveal the party information: Use red construction paper, black marker, a hole punch, and a paper fastener. Cut two 6" × 4½" ovals from red paper. Trim ½" all around one oval, for the body. Cut 2" from one end of the second oval, then cut it in half lengthwise, for two wings. Overlap the wings on the body, aligning the outside edges, and punch a hole through all layers. Insert a paper fastener. Blacken the head, leaving eyes and a smile, and mark big spots on the wings. Under the wings, write the party information.

Decorations

- Give kids a bug's eye view of the world: Begin with a big roll of green paper and cut deep zigzags along one edge for grass. Tape it along one wall or all around the party area. If you wish, ask your small fry to color bugs on the grass before you tape it up.
- Make giant flowers from colorful crêpe paper or

tissue paper fanned out around paper-plate centers. Add crêpe streamer stems of various lengths. Add huge paper leaves. Affix these flowers to the walls with double-sided foam tape (picture mounts), which won't mar the paint if removed carefully.

Party Starters

Antennae and Wings

Hand out deely-boppers—those foam balls that extend on coiled wire from hairbands. You can find them at party stores or mail order houses. Let kids draw on big, symmetrical shapes cut from large sheets of folded poster board to make their own colorful butterfly or dragonfly wings. These can be tied or taped on their backs.

Crafty Caterpillar

Beforehand: Cut each of several egg cartons into two lengthwise rows of egg holders, and pierce two holes at one end with a pencil point.

At the party: Let kids push pipe cleaners through the holes to make antennae, and glue on wiggle eyes. Smiles, dots, and stripes can be added, using crayons on plastic-foam egg cartons, washable markers on the paper variety.

PARENTS ALERT

This project snares even the shyest guest, but young toddlers who still put things in their mouths should not use the pipe cleaners and wiggle eyes—help them draw on features instead.

Activities

Buzzing Around

With kids sitting in a circle, play the traditional game of duck, duck, goose with the words "bug, bug, butterfly," or perhaps "buzz, buzz, bee!" (If you're not familiar with the game, talk to any nursery school teacher.)

Wiggle and Squirm

Play a recording of some lively children's music. Have the kids form a conga line and imitate a giant centipede, then drop to the ground and creep like an inchworm.

Race and Trap

Beforehand: Make a few big bugs. First wad up newspaper into three balls and tape the balls together to form the head and body (thorax and abdomen). Then tape on big paper wings.

To play: Divide the kids into pairs or trios and, using soft elastic or scarves, tie together the legs of each set of kids as you would for a three-legged race. Tell them they're now spiders. Ask the kids to run a short distance, grab a "bug," and trap it in their web by wrapping it completely in toilet paper. The youngest kids will be happy to just snare the bug; skip the toilet paper step.

Water Bugs

If climate allows for an outdoor party and bare feet, this game makes a big splash. Early in the day, fill lots of balloons with water, knot the ends, and use a felt-tip marker to add some bug features, such as big eyes, antennae, and wings. Pair the kids up and put them in two lines, opposite their partners. The distance between the lines depends on the age of the kids. Partners throw and catch water balloons back and forth, until the balloons drop and break. The last balloon left intact belongs to the winning team. Kids will want to play this game two or three times, so have plenty of water bugs on hand. (If water balloons are out of the question, make quick bean-bag bugs using inexpensive socks. Any sock that is dropped is "out.") If your guests are too young to be able to throw and catch, have them roll a large ball back and forth between the lines of partners.

PARENTS ALERT

Be sure to immediately discard the broken balloons. Have towels on hand in case anyone gets splashed.

Food

Bumblebee Cupcakes

Start with cupcakes made from scratch or a mix. Cover them with vanilla frosting, then dip each in a bowl of yellow sugar crystals. For the bee's head, cut a marshmallow in half horizontally and dip the cut edge in the same crystals. Use brown decorator icing to adhere the head to one side of a cupcake top, and to add mini-marshmallow eyeballs and a sugar cookie cut in half for wings. Also dot the eyeballs and draw a smiling mouth and stripes with the icing. One-inch strands of black string licorice make great antennae. Insert a chocolate kiss for a stinger.

Also serve apple slices to dip into bowls of honey and, of course, fruit punch in a pitcher labeled "beetle juice."

Story Time

The Very Hungry Caterpillar by Eric Carle (Putnam). A growing caterpillar munches through the pages!

The Very Quiet Cricket by Eric Carle (Putnam). Everything else about this story is noisy!

The Ants and the Grasshopper, from any book of Aesop's fables, showcases a real contrast of characters and entertains children of all ages.

Spider on the Floor by Bill Russell (Crown). In this Raffi (children's singer/songwriter) Songs to Read book, a spider wreaks havoc.

Party Favor

Make bug jars, using jelly jars or clear plastic food containers with holes punched in the lids; or use mason jars with removable lid centers, which you replace with a same-size circle cut from vinyl mesh canvas. Personalize each container by writing a child's name on it with a paint pen. You might fill the container with gummy worms, a spider ring, a temporary tattoo, a "sticky" window-walker insect, a metal cricket that clicks, or for girls, a butterfly barrette. Explain that kids could use their bug jars to catch lightning bugs, or they could put a caterpillar and some leaves inside and watch the co-cooning process.

PARENTS ALERT

If you punch holes in the jar lids, turn them over and flatten the rough edges with a small hammer.

The Berry Patch

Treat your child to a berry happy birthday! Haven't you heard? Berries are the "currant" rage. OK, you may have to plant the seeds for such a trend. Girls and boys-'n-berries 3 to 5 years old will find this a juicy theme.

Invitation

Write "Come on over to the berry patch for Sonya's 4th birthday!" on card-stock paper. Punch a hole and insert the shank of a strawberry button from the fabric store. Insert a small piece of pipe cleaner through the hole in the shank to secure it in place.

Decorations

- Hang garlands or vines wired with artificial berries at the doorway or over the windows.
- Fill vases with sprigs of artificial berries; place them along the center of the table. Be sure the berries are firmly attached to their stems so that kids won't try to eat them.
- Purchase three red helium-filled balloons to secure at the mailbox or front entrance to your house. Turn them into strawberries: With a black felt-tip marker, mark polka dots all over to represent seeds. On top of each balloon, glue a star of green felt (a hull) and a rolled-up tube of the same felt (a stem).

Party Starters

Juice Writing

Put out white paper and inexpensive paintbrushes. Put some berries in a plastic plate; let the kids squash the berries with a potato masher and then paint with the juice.

Extraordinary Berry Baskets

If you haven't collected these and hoarded them, ask your grocer for a stash at a minimal price. If they're the old-fashioned wood baskets or paper-pulp containers, give kids washable markers to draw all over them. If they're the plastic mesh type, let kids weave all sorts of items through the latticework: strands of ribbons and yarn, pipe cleaners, bumpy chenille sticks, quilling paper, twisted paper—assign an older sibling to help.

Activities

Berry Picking

Throw jumbo pom-poms in red (strawberries), blue (blueberries), and black (blackberries) all over the floor. Challenge the kids to pick up all three types of berry in each hand before they can put any in their berry basket. This takes coordination! Repeat the challenge until no pom-poms are left.

Blueberry Toss

> Beforehand: Make up some "blueberry" bean bags using two 4"-diameter circles of navy blue felt for each. Sew or glue the edges together,

leaving an inch or two open until you insert
some small dried beans with a funnel. (These
would make great party favors!) Let kids aim
for three bushel baskets, set up various short
distances away. On one, draw a blueberry pie
and a 3 for the points it earns; on another, draw
a blueberry muffin and a 2; and on the last, a
blueberry pancake, worth 1 point.

"Berried" Treasure

Hide big plastic strawberries, plastic spoons, and a few
other plastic trinkets in a sandbox and invite kids to keep
what they find.

Food

Berry Delicious Sandwiches

Prepare crustless sandwiches with seedless raspberry or
blueberry jelly.

Berry au Lait

Mix milk with strawberry-flavored powder or syrup.

Berry Sweets

- Purchase or make a pound cake loaf or an angel
  food cake. Top with whipped cream and whatever
  berries are available, in season, and acceptable to
  the kids.
- Make thumbprint cookies with berry jelly of some
  kind in the center; serve with raspberry ice cream
  or sherbet.

PARENTS ALERT
Strawberries are a common allergen for young children. To be safe, leave strawberries off the menu.

Story Time

Blueberries for Sal by Robert McCloskey (Viking Press). While they're eating blueberries, a little girl and a bear cub lose their respective mothers, and almost end up with the wrong ones.

Jamberry by Bruce Degen (Harpercrest). A boy and a bear go on a berry-picking adventure in Berryland.

Party Favor

Kids can carry berrious goodies home in their berry baskets: a blueberry beanbag; a scratch 'n' sniff sticker; strawberry-scented potpourri bundled up in a square of strawberry-print fabric; a strawberry- or cherry-flavored lollipop; and the "berried" treasures they found.

Construction Site

Constructive imaginations build their own excitement! There are countless 3- to 6-year-olds who love to assemble houses, bridges, magic castles, and machines. So here's to big powerful trucks, unbelievable edifices, and a towering good time.

Invitation
From heavy paper make a dump truck cutout with a dumper that tilts to reveal the party information. Write "Haul yourself over for Tim's birthday!" on the cab door.

Decorations
- At party stores you can probably find a roll of plastic strip printed with bold, diagonal yellow and black stripes, similar to the caution-alerts and "keep out" tape used at real construction sites. If not, purchase bright surveyor's tape at a hardware store. Unroll the strip or tape and secure it all around the party zone.
- Post signs you block-letter yourself: "Under Construction," "Pardon Our Mess," "Party in Progress."
- Cover the table with clean brown paper to simulate dirt. Top with a few large toy trucks—Tonka dump trucks are a great example—which hold snack food.

Party Starters

Cracker Stacks

Pass out plastic hard hats, just to get kids in the mood. Set out lots of graham crackers and piles of small gumdrops. Challenge the kids to erect their own architectural frameworks using these supplies. Expect that some of the building materials will never make it into construction.

Activities

Busy Builders

Using construction toys or building units of any kind, let the kids free-build. You go, guys! Have a camera ready to take snapshots.

Building Contests

For older kids, announce a building-unit competition for work crews (OK, kid partnerships), such as who can build the tallest tower or whose bridge can withstand the most weight before falling down.

Put the Dirt in the Dump Truck

Beforehand: Enlarge the invitation design to giant proportions. Cut irregular mounds of dirt from brown paper.

At the party: Let blindfolded kids play this as they would Pin the Tail on the Donkey, using double-sided tape to attach the paper dirt to the dumper.

Morphing Machines

Instruct the kids to imagine themselves to be big trucks. They may roll over and over to become cement mixers, somersault forward as steamrollers, get down on all fours and arch backs as dump trucks. What does a fork-lift look like? A cherry picker? A crane? Can you be a front-end loader? You can set this up like follow-the-leader, let the kids work in pairs, have them all morph at once, or play it like charades.

Food

Sweet Site

After admiring the construction site in miniature atop this birthday cake, the kids will probably be more into demolition than anything else. Start by baking a sheet cake—banana cake will provide a wonderfully tex-tural foundation for this creation. Frost (tint the frost-ing grass-green or earth-brown), then sprinkle brown sugar "soil" all over the top, mounding up a pile in the center. Use a spatula to bulldoze roads into the soil. Park clean mini trucks over the site: a dump truck, a front-end loader, maybe a backhoe or cement mixer. Add a few stacked gumdrop shrubs. Look for candles or candleholders that look like mini construction cones.

Story Time

  Mike Mulligan and His Steam Shovel by Vir-ginia Lee Burton (Houghton Mifflin). Mike proves the usefulness of his old equipment.

Machines at Work by Byron Barton (Crowell).
Watch as a building gets knocked down and a
new one is started in its place.

Party Favor

For each child, put together a kit for their next construction job. Include a sheet of sandpaper for a base, a mini
truck, some chalk for surveying, and a box of raisins or
a package of chocolate-covered raisins for a "rock pile."
Pack everything in a lunch pail or lunch box—or a paper
take-out container—with the child's name on it. Parents
will love bringing this kit when the family goes to a
slow-food restaurant.

AGED TO PERFECTION

	1-year-olds	2-year-olds
Number of guests	2	3
Optimal ratio of adults to children	1 to 1	1 to 1
Length of party	1 hour	1 to 1½ hours
Great goody bags	Bibs; bright-colored sipping cups; big balls, each individualized with a child's name	Pails and shovels, each with a child's name written on it; crayons; coloring books
Fun foods	Small pieces of banana; ice cream; miniature waffles	Ice cream in small paper cups; finger sandwiches
Favorite games	Pat-a-cake; "The Itsy-Bitsy Spider"; catch with rolling balls	"Ring around the Rosy"; "London Bridge is Falling Down"; make a parade
Safety tips	Make sure all balloons are blown up. Throw away popped ones immediately, or stick with Mylar balloons.	
	For children under 2, enclose the party area with gates. Leave space for running.	
	Be sure foods do not present a choking hazard. Remove anything breakable. Tie draperies back and tape down electrical wires.	

3- and 4-year-olds	5- and 6-year-olds	7- to 10-year-olds
4 to 5	6 to 7	8 to 11
1 to 3	1 to 4	1 to 5
1½ hours	1½ to 2½ hours	2 to 3 hours
Stickers; play clay; crayons and coloring books; Slinky spiral-spring toys	Jump ropes; sidewalk chalk; marbles; costume jewelry; miniature flashlights	Key chains; baseball cards; erasers; anything slimy; hats
Bite-size vegetable strips and yogurt dip; wafer ice cream cones; miniature rice cakes	Apples on a stick; pizza; foot-long hot dogs; fresh popcorn	Pizza; make-your-own sundaes; chocolate-dipped apples and bananas
Duck, duck, goose; pin-the-tail-on-the-donkey; freeze dance	Simon says; tag; treasure hunt; limbo; hot potato; 20 questions	Scavenger hunt; bingo; bubble-gum blowing contest; limbo
Lock or disconnect VCRs, tempting exercise equipment, and stereos.		Remove matches; cake knife, and other sharp objects when you've finished using them.

Barnyard Bash

A farm-theme party lets everyone make hay—rain or shine. A simulated farm provides urban and suburban children with bushels of fun; 3- to 6-year-old hayseeds will be talking about this party 'til the cows come home! If you can, provide some bales of straw; small fry love climbing and balancing on them. Suggest that everyone (grown-ups included) wear overalls.

Invitation

For each guest, cut out a simple barn shape from red construction paper; cut a T-shaped slit for double doors. On a piece of white paper, draw the outline of the barn with the doors open. Write the party particulars inside the door outline and photocopy as necessary. Cut out the white barns and glue one behind each red barn.

Decorations

- Place a welcoming scarecrow near the door. Use a pillowcase for the head and old clothes for the body; stuff with straw or wadded newspaper. Use twine or safety pins to assemble the components.
- Make a smiling cow. To begin, tape or glue an empty plastic soda bottle to the top of one end of a sawhorse. Drape an oval of felt decorated with large spots over the sawhorse; slit the felt so it slips over the soda bottle. To make the head, tie the corners of

a pillowcase with twine to form ears, then stuff the case and tie closed with twine. Cut a muzzle and other features from felt; tape or glue them to the pillowcase. Slide the pillowcase over the soda bottle, adjusting the twine tie as necessary.
- Cover the table with gingham or burlap fabric.
- Bales of hay, baskets, buckets, watering cans, and milk cans all set the mooooo-d.

Party Starters

Milk Pail Keepsakes
Give each child a miniature milk pail to decorate with stickers of barnyard images. Have a bandanna in the pail and tie it around the child's neck or tuck it in a pocket.

Activities

Egg Hunt
Hide plastic eggs around the party area and let the kids search for them and put them in their pails. If you like, use eggs that open and place a favor in each first.

Spoon Race
For this relay, divide kids into teams and give each team a large spoon and an egg—plastic, wood, or hard-boiled. Without touching the team egg at all, each child must carry the egg on the spoon forward and back along a course, then pass the egg to the next person on the team.

Hayrides

Line several wagons with straw or blankets. Put one or two kids in each and ask older siblings or other parents to pull the wagons gently around the yard; end up at the sawhorse cow. Set each child astride the cow and take his picture.

Square Dancing

Ask at the library for a tape or a video that explains some simple movements, such as do-si-do and à-la-main left. Let the kids link arms and twirl.

Food

Haystacks

In a bowl toss together thin snacks such as potato sticks and pretzel sticks. Arrange them in a pile on each child's plate.

The Vegetable Patch

Serve a tray of raw veggies kids love, such as baby carrots, broccoli florets, celery sticks, cherry tomatoes, green beans, and canned baby corn. Line 'em up to look like a big garden.

PARENTS ALERT
Veggies sliced into coins are a choking hazard for children under 5, so be sure to leave them whole or cut them into sticks.

Pigs-in-a-Poke

For each, roll one to two slices of sandwich meat and place the meat in a frankfurter roll; top with a slice of cheese. Bake in a 350°F oven for 10 minutes. Serve warm; have mustard and ketchup on the table.

Barnyard Cake

Frost a square or rectangular cake with milk chocolate frosting. Divide the cake into penned areas, using fences from the craft store. Install a little garden of green gum-drops, into which you insert the birthday candles. Rows of candy pumpkins would be dandy. Add crumbled wheat-biscuit cereal mixed with sugar for hay, brown sugar crystals for chicken feed, and green sprinkles for grass. Set small plastic farm animals around all but the crop areas.

Story Time

Farm Days by William Wegman (Hyperion Press). This photographer dresses up his beloved weimaraners to tell the story of the city dog who visits his country cousins.

Old MacDonald Had a Farm. Kids will sing along to any edition of this book as they view a farm couple's very hectic day.

Party Favor

Kids will go hog-wild over any of these parting gifts, carried home in their milk pails: collected eggs; a plastic animal from the cake; an eraser, nail brush, or soap in the shape of sheep, pig, or cow; a farm-animal noise-maker; the bandanna.

"IT WORKED FOR ME"

"Part of the fun of my son's birthday parties is the surprise element. Kids never know what to expect! But my daughter seems more comfortable when she knows just what's coming, and I've found that I need to go over the agenda with her repeatedly."

Castle Kingdom

Create a happily-ever-after memory for your little prince or princess. Children 3 to 7 years old will best appreciate this royal treatment. For a medieval coronation procession, put out a bunch of old clothes, with slips and skirts for long gowns and shirts to tie on by their sleeves for capes. Then have the knights and ladies don hats and crowns they make. Poof! You've got photo opportunities galore.

Invitation

Write a proclamation: "Hear ye, hear ye! Come to Sophie's Kingdom to celebrate her birthday!" and add the date, time, and address of the party. Photocopy the proclamation on parchmentlike paper. Roll up each into a scroll and tie it with royal blue ribbon. If you can't hand these out personally, use mailing tubes to send them.

Decorations

- For pennants, cut out rectangles from colorful felt, paper, or cloth, then cut notches at one end and suspend them with string around the party area.
- Make cardboard swords, covered with aluminum foil, and cross them over doorways.
- Drape royal blue and gold star garlands along the table and sprinkle fake jewels around.
- Decorate a big chair with foil and streamers for the birthday child's "throne."

Party Starters

Announce each guest as "Sir Harry" or "the Duchess of
Wilson, Lady Jennifer!" Use a homemade megaphone
decorated lavishly with aluminum foil and ribbon
streamers.

Shields

Beforehand: Cut brightly colored poster board
into 10" × 15" pieces, then taper one end of
each to form a shield shape. Use a wide marker
to draw lines dividing it diagonally into halves
or thirds, or vertically and horizontally into
quadrants, so kids will have more than one area
to decorate.

Staple wide elastic across the center of the
back for a handhold: The elastic should lie flat
against the poster board and be as long as necessary to be secured by the stapler; cover the staples on both sides of the shield with cloth tape.
Set out markers or crayons, glue, stickers,
crêpe-paper streamers, and margarine tubs of
precut felt or craft-foam shapes. If all the guests
are over 5, you can put out tubs of spangles, sequins, and fake jewels, too.

At the party: Ask the kids to decorate their shields
by designing a personal coat of arms with pictures of items important to the child.

Crowns and Hats

Purchase paper crowns and cone-shaped party hats at a
party store. Have the kids decorate these along with, or
instead of, the shields.

Activities

The Crowning Touch

Blow up small balloons ahead of time. Give each child a crown to wear. Divide the kids into pairs and have one child throw a balloon to his partner, who tries to catch it in the crown on her head. Even easier: Have the kids try to catch undecorated crowns on balloons with faces you've drawn on them.

PARENTS ALERT

This game is suitable for kids 4 and older; younger children can try to catch a crown on a large ball or teddy bear. Be sure to promptly discard any balloons that break or deflate.

Fight the Dragon

Disguise a purchased dinosaur piñata (available at party stores) as a dragon by gluing craft foam scales down the back and a tissue-paper flame in the mouth. Fill it with goodies and then suspend it from a branch or doorway. Give each child a chance to slay the dragon, holding a shield and a purchased plastic sword, or a plastic baseball bat "lance." Or, disguise a dinosaur toy as a dragon, suspend it with a long rope slung over a tree branch, and have an older child or an adult control the tension on the rope, letting the dragon bite the dust for each valiant knight and then raising it again for the next contestant.

Into the Moat

Have the kids play the classic tug-of-war over a blanket "moat." Give each team a kingdom, or pit the dragons against the knights, or the wizards against the jesters, aiming for a fair distribution of sizes on each side.

In the Throne Room

Here's a benevolent version of musical chairs. Instead of using one less chair than children and eliminating players, use the same number of chairs, lined up and facing alternate directions. Include in the line-up that special chair you've decorated like a throne (or simply tape a crown cutout to a high-backed chair). Play the music while kids make a procession around the chairs. Stop the music abruptly while kids grab the nearest chair. The child who happens to be seated upon the throne is declared king or queen, and awarded a gold (chocolate) coin or plastic jewel. Play a few rounds, or until everyone has been coronated—easy enough for the disc jockey to control.

Food

Magic Potion

Mix a packet of brightly colored, unsweetened drink mix with 1½ cups of water, and pour into an ice cube tray. Repeat with another color/flavor mix. Freeze until solid. At the party, drop one or two ice cubes into lemon-lime carbonated soda. As the cubes melt, the sparkling drink will be transformed!

The King's Fare

Begin with sliced bread from which you have trimmed the crust, layer with your child's favorite filling, and then notch one end to resemble a crown.

The Queen's Jewels

Make cherry, lemon, and blueberry gelatin in shallow pans, and cut each into diamond shapes.

Castle Cake

Start with a double-layer square cake. (Avoid a recipe with pudding, so that you won't need to refrigerate this lofty project.) Ice the cake with white or stone-color icing. Then, using decorator icing squeezed from tubes, adhere ice cream cone towers and turrets, mini marshmallows, cookie and candy details, and outline windows. Graham crackers and string licorice make a great drawbridge! Before the icing sets completely, sprinkle on multicolored sugar crystals for a magical touch. Glue paper pennants on toothpicks and insert these at the highest points.

Story Time

May I Bring a Friend? by Beatrice Schenk de Regniers (Atheneum). A little boy brings an animal friend each time he visits the king and queen for tea—with hilarious results.

Arthur and the Sword by Robert Sabuda (Aladdin Paperbacks). Magnificent, stained-glass images enhance this story about young King Arthur and his sword, Excalibur.

Party Favor

A mini knight figure on horseback or little plastic unicorn is a great take-home gift. Or, fill a plastic goblet with a king's ransom: gold chocolate coins and other metallic-wrapped candies. The crowns, hats, and shields the children decorated are party favors, too!

Tea Party

Your high-society tyke will relish a birthday tea. Teatime is for dress-up, for pretending to be grown-up, and feeling so very special. Its mock fanciness appeals to many kids—even as young as 3—who enjoy a pleasant change from their everyday routine. Give older siblings the important role of waiter or waitress, in charge of gentle and elegant service. If your guest list is small, why not invite the parents to join you for tea as well?

Invitation

Make a double-layer paper teacup shape and glue all but the top edges together. Make a paper "tea bag" to fit inside the cup and on it write a formal invitation: "Kindly join us for a tea party in honor of Katie's 5th birthday." Add the party particulars, tape a string to the back, and insert the invitation into the cup. Ask children to dress like grown-ups, suggesting hats, ties, gloves, and jewelry. Also request that they bring a favorite doll or stuffed animal to introduce into society.

Decorations

- A separate little table for the dolls the kids brought, with white freezer paper for a table covering and little cups of crayons
- White tablecloths
- Pretty paperware

- Paper doilies under the cakes and cookies
- Fresh or artificial flowers in bud vases

Party Starters

Ask children to present their dolls and stuffed animals to one or more guests, and explain their origins and the reasons for their names. Children can use crayons at the toys' table to create place settings, or place pictures of food you've cut from magazines beforehand on small, paper dessert plates.

Activities

"T" is for Treasure Hunt

Enlarge and photocopy our playing card or a similar card, and tape one to a shopping bag for each child. Beforehand, hide all the items shown on the card so that each child may find all six items. (Use fruit tea that small sophisticates will enjoy.) Assemble younger children into tea(m)s, each with an older maître d' to assist them.

Sing-along

Lead some songs (or play tapes) that the kids can act out the lyrics to: "I'm a Little Teapot," "Be My Guest" from *Beauty and the Beast*, "Tea for Two," and other greatest hits.

Teacup Tower

Have little ladies and gents construct stacks of alternating teacups and saucers—all paper goods, of course. See whose tower is tallest before it tumbles down.

Food

Tea Sandwiches

On one type of bread spread butter, peanut butter, jelly, cream cheese, and/or thin cucumber slices, and top with a different type of bread, for a three-tone effect. Cut out the sandwiches with cookie cutters.

Suits-Me-to-a-Tea Cakes

Add 1 tablespoon of lemon juice or 1 teaspoon of lemon extract to a plain cake mix. Bake in a mini muffin pan, with paper liners. Using tinted frosting, ice each cupcake. Arrange the cakes on a doily-lined platter and top each with a candle; after blowing out the candles, the birthday child (or one of the waitstaff) can pass one to each guest. Offer a buffet of various toppings: mini chocolate chips, rainbow sprinkles, colored sugar crystals, and other sprinkle or icing decorations from the baking supply aisle of the supermarket. Let each child decorate a little tea cake to her liking.

Just My Cup of Fruited Tea

Mix mint tea with orange juice or lemonade. Serve cold from a teapot into paper cups with handles.

Story Time

Miss Spider's Tea Party by David Kirk (Scholastic). One of a popular series of books starring Miss Spider.

The Mad Hatter's Tea Party from Alice in Wonderland; any edition by Lewis Carroll or an adaptation.

Party Favor

Make a gourmet tea package: Purchase inexpensive but
interesting plastic cups or mugs—look for animal motifs, like a giraffe whose neck stretches to form the handle, or opt for pretty printed "grown-up" decoration. Fill
each cup with after-dinner candies or other bite-size
snacks, wrapped in colorful cellophane or a doily. Place
each mug in a colorful gift bag, fold down the top, and
secure with a gold sticker.

CONTINGENCY PLANS

**Good planning is essential—including planning for
the unexpected. An activity you thought would take
10 minutes might require 30. More often, it will fizzle
after 5. To be safe, plan more activities than you
think you'll need.**

12 Emergency Activities

- If the children are old enough to play catch, they'll
  love a quick game of keep-the-balloon-in-the-air. If
  the kids are under 5, be sure to remove the balloons
  as soon as the game is over.

- Let the children make chalk drawings on the sidewalk.

- Before the kids arrive, hide foil-wrapped candies in
  your party area. If you need to, you can have a
  quick treasure hunt.

- Divide the children into teams. Give each team an ice cube. See which team can melt it the quickest. . . . without putting it in anyone's mouth!

- Fill a jar with jelly beans. Ask each child to guess how many beans are in it. The one who comes closest gets the jar!

- Hold a bean-bag race. Have the children walk to a goal while balancing the bags on their heads. If a bag drops, that child has to start again.

- Freeze dance works for all ages. Turn on the music and kids dance. Turn it off, and kids "freeze." The first person who moves before the music comes back on must sit out the next round, but he can help you monitor the other kids for their "freezing" endurance.

- Cut apples in half horizontally. For older kids, cut straight. For younger kids, make the cuts distinctive: zigzags and curves. Give each child one half. Have the kids find their apple "mate." They'll probably work up an apple-tite!

- Play telephone. Have the children sit in a row or circle. One child quickly whispers a message to the next, who whispers it to the next, and so forth. The message travels down the line until the last child says it out loud.

CONTINGENCY PLANS

Usually the message has changed considerably and hilariously!

- Play familiar games, such as duck, duck, goose or "Ring around the Rosy," if you see young kids getting overstimulated or cranky.

- A classic game of tag is always a winner when kids need to let off steam.

- Sing. Little kids love "Where is Thumpkin?" and other hand songs. Older kids can sing favorites as loud and as soft as possible!

Road Race

Ready, set, go supersonic with a Birthday 500 flash-and-dash party. This bash is a sure bet for 4- to 6-year-olds—both for kids with energy to burn and for quiet kids who will get their engines revved. Ask kids to bring their bike helmets, and if everyone has in-line or roller skates, you might incorporate these into the games. For older kids, explore your local area for slot-car racing and book a track so that the kids can race the electronically operated model cars.

Invitation

Cut out a magazine picture of a race car or sports car and glue it to postcard-size paper. Glue your child's mug-shot photo in the driver's seat. Next to the child's face draw a bubble frame and write "Race on over to my party!" inside it. Make color copies to glue onto postcards. Write the party particulars on or next to the car before photocopying, or put them on the message side of the postcard.

Decorations

- Post traffic signs made from yellow, red, and green poster board around the party area. Borrow cones from the gym teacher at school, or fashion your own from orange poster board.
- Hang black and white checkerboard racing flags (from a party store), or purchase a similar material

from a fabric store, cut it into rectangles, and glue the edges over string.

- Crisscross the table with roads made from strips of brown paper; apply white tape to delineate lanes. Park a pullback car for a party favor at each place setting. (Kids will have a great time at this table.)
- Make wearable race cars for each child: Cut a hole in the bottom of a cardboard produce box, making it just large enough for your child to slip over his head and slide down to his waist. Remove any flaps and turn the box over so the hole is at the top. Cover the box with assorted colors of self-adhesive vinyl. For wheels, position four 10" plastic plates on the sides, pierce holes in the center, and insert paper fasteners. Make handholds by cutting a 1" × 3" slot between the wheels. To make headlights, glue two 6" white paper bowls to the front of the box. Have the child step into the car and pull it up. Or, for an easier take on this getup, make front bumpers only from strips of cardboard, adding headlights as described above. Tie a length of ribbon around each bumper behind each headlight, place a bumper against each child's tummy, and then tie the ribbons together at the back of his waist. Make these especially for any siblings or guests under 4 who won't be able to hold up a complete sedan.

Party Starters

Creative License

These personalized license plates really drive up kids' self-esteem. They'll want to hang them around their necks as they race through the games and then later hang them on their bedroom door.

You need:
- 9" × 12" sheets of craft foam in assorted colors, two per child
- A bag of precut craft-foam shapes
- An assortment of buttons, flat acrylic jewels, and spangles
- Satin cord, 27" length for each
- Squeeze bottles of craft glue
- Permanent felt-tip marker or paint pen
- 2"-high stencils for block, capital letters
- Scissors, hole punch

Beforehand: Prepare the basic license plate and the cutout shapes. First, cut half the craft foam sheets crosswise in half and round the corners. On one piece, cut away the center, leaving a ½" frame all around. Glue this frame to a piece of foam in a contrasting color. When the glue is dry, use a hole punch to make two holes in the top edge of the license plate. From the remaining craft foam, cut out small rectangles and write the name of a state on each one; also cut out letters for each child's name.

At the party: Let each child find the letters of his name, arrange them across a license plate, and then add assorted decorations. Have him glue everything down and leave it to dry for about 15 minutes. He can then thread the ends of the satin cord through the holes in the plate and tie the ends together.

Activities

Let the kids wear their helmets, race-car getups, and license plates to drive themselves through an exciting racecourse:

Crazy-8

Set up a figure-eight course, using traffic cones, sidewalk chalk, or other guides. Use a stopwatch to clock everyone's time around the course.

Hot Rod Relays

Divide the kids into teams and see which team is fastest. Use obstacles or require jumping, hopping, or keeping tires—er, feet, on the ground at all times, or any other variation. Instead of the wearable cars, give each team a hula hoop that each team member must roll to a goal, around it, and back.

Red Light, Green Light

In this classic game, a "traffic cop," with his back to the others, announces "Green light" or holds up giant green GO sign, while the pint-size race-car drivers head down a course toward him. At any given moment, the traffic cop turns around, yells "Red light!" and perhaps turns the sign around to the red STOP sign side. Drivers must immediately freeze or go back to the start. The first to reach the traffic cop takes over the job.

To get off the fast track, switch gears and organize another type of activity:

Little Streaks o' Lightning
Have the kids race pull-back party favor cars on a smooth surface.

Squirt Power
Let the kids race lightweight plastic cars down a course to a line of tape, pushing each with a stream of water from a squirt bottle. In case a waterfight (car wash?) breaks out, this race would be best held outdoors in warm weather.

Food

RPM (Real Party Macaroni)
Any macaroni dish is bound to be a winner as long as it features wheel pasta throughout! Choose a salad at room temperature or a hot macaroni-and-cheese casserole, as the season or the birthday child indicates.

Racetrack Snacks
Serve pretzels and raw veggies in inverted helmets lined with plastic wrap.

PARENTS ALERT

Don't cut the veggies into coin-size pieces; these are choking hazards.

Premium Fuel

Select any beverage that gives kids a little sugar for energy. Serve two kinds; place in pitchers labeled "regular" and "high test."

Race Car Crullers

Let guests assemble their own edible race cars. Set out components as follows, along with decorator icing for "glue" and detailing. Crullers (stick donuts) form the car body, round cookies the wheels, little pieces of graham crackers the windshield. Add candies for the steering wheel, head and taillights, and fenders. When it's time to eat them, put a number candle in the driver's seat of the birthday child's model.

Story Time

The Berenstain Bears and the Big Road Race by Stan and Jan Berenstain (Random House). Kids learn colors and fair play as this exciting race proceeds.

The Tortoise and the Hare. The classic race in any collection of Aesop's fables.

Party Favor

Traffic Light: A black paper bag to which you've glued a red, yellow, and green circle. Insert a key chain, a portable game like travel bingo, or an activity book for car trips. When it's time to cross the finish line, let the kids add the mini car from the table—and, of course, their creative licenses.

"IT WORKED FOR ME"

"Although the party started and ended at our house, we took the kids on a field trip—to the police station. They loved spending a few seconds in jail!"

HAPPY BIRTHDAY PARTYERS

Boost their confidence, build their self-esteem, and reward their good behavior! You'll get a high return for your investment: cheerful attitudes and smiling faces. Happy guests will also make the birthday child feel like a million bucks. Here are some tips to make it all happen:

Plan

- Take your child's and your family's needs into account when you set the date and time for the party. If your half-pint or his friend nap in the afternoon, a morning party may be best. If your child is not a good eater, don't try to have a party at a time when a meal will be expected. Also, make sure the party won't interfere with a friend's birthday party or a sibling's soccer practice.

HAPPY BIRTHDAY PARTYERS

- Limit the number of children you invite. The rule of thumb is to invite one child more than the birthday kid's age. For example, if your child is turning 5, invite up to six guests. (See Aged to Perfection, pages 38–39.) Any more and you won't be able to keep track of each kid's emotional needs. You want to be able to notice if anyone is holding back from participating or is not comfortable with the foods you're offering.

- Ask guests' parents to let you know of any food allergies at RSVP time. Don't let these spoil your child's selection of treats, but try to provide some alternatives—for instance, a choice of nondairy ice cream for lactose-intolerant kids. To be safe, keep strawberries and nuts off the menu.

- Pace the party to keep the kids' interest, make things lively, and provide short breaks. As a general rule of thumb, think about changing the activity or the type of activity at least every 20 minutes.

- Be age appropriate: if you select activities in keeping with your child's stage of development, her day will go smoothly. Most of the parties in this book will appeal to children at a range of ages, but some are of course most appropriate for toddlers or grade-schoolers. The introductory paragraph that accompanies each party indicates the target age, but don't hesitate to adapt a theme up or down.

- Plan more games and activities than you'll need. You'll be prepared in case one activity isn't developmentally right for the group, and avoid letting it go on to the point where kids become frustrated. For ideas, see Contingency Plans, page 54.

- Avoid elimination games, like musical chairs. Likewise, stay away from designating team captains who take turns choosing the members of their teams from among the group. These activities are always hard on someone's ego.

- Think about using place cards at the table. This formal nicety heads off any disputes on who sits where, and who gets to sit next to whom.

- After refreshments, older kids will want time for opening gifts, but younger children will need an activity to occupy them until they are picked up. Another story, another game, or repeating a game the kids enjoyed—each of these "fillers" might end the party on a good note. Take some time to think about what activities to do with that last lingering guest whose parent is late.

HAPPY BIRTHDAY PARTYERS

Party

- Greet everyone in a special, attentive way. Make each guest feel wanted and important. Say goodbye in a similar way.

- Kids love seeing their names in print. Writing their names on badges, place cards, or party favors makes them feel important.

- Let kids know your ground rules early on. For example, you might announce, "Just three rules, kids: no jumping on the furniture, take turns, and have fun." Understanding the limitations from the beginning will save them the humiliation of scoldings later.

- Keep kids busy and challenged. Start with a creative activity to involve the kids as soon as they arrive. Look for icebreakers—like our Party Starters—that make shy kids comfortable. Guests won't have time for self-consciousness or mischief.

- Guide the activities. Establish a "safety zone" and explain that the game stops at its borders and anyone who wants to opt out of an activity can step into this area at any time. When establishing pairs, buddies, or teams, try to match the size and energy levels of participants so that small kids won't be overwhelmed by bigger partners.

- Opening presents is best left out of a party for very young children. It's hard for young children to share brand-new toys, and it's hard for those who are not getting the presents to sit and watch. Some experts advise that for children under 6, you should avoid potential conflicts and open presents after the party.

- Let a child aged 6 or over open presents at the end of a party. Make sure you've rehearsed your child on gift acceptance speeches beforehand. If possible, ask another adult to record the gifts, so that you can devote yourself to praising the gift and the giver, coaxing the proper thank you's from your child if necessary, and greeting parents arriving to collect their children.

Reward

- If your child's friends don't have the best manners, reward anything close to good behavior. After a while, close-to-good will turn into great. Little trinkets, tickets to collect and redeem, or even tiny candies give kids a reason to be good.

- Have an awards ceremony at the end of the party and find some reason to give an award to every single child.

- Move gracefully into the final good-byes as guests leave. The party favor or goody bag is a consolation prize to resign kids to the idea of going home.

HAPPY BIRTHDAY PARTYERS

Trust your Instincts
At all times, be perceptive to the kids' attentions and behaviors. Knowing when to divert from the original plan keeps a party interesting, varied, and running smoothly. Most important, keep the pace relaxed. Remind yourself and the kids that it's a party, and just for fun.

"IT WORKED FOR ME"

"I write down every activity in the order we planned on a 3" × 5" card. On the back, I list some extra emergency activities. I carry this little reference in my pocket during the whole party, so I won't forget anything."

Firefighter's 5-Alarm Party

Fire kids up with a red-hot celebration! The plethora of party goods available for this theme proves that it has spread like wildfire and remains hot, especially for 4- to 6-year-olds. Provide a plastic fire helmet for each guest and ask each to bring a slicker (borrow a few extra, just in case). If you can, arrange for the kids to take a tour of your local firehouse. If not, offer a glimpse into firefighting via picture books or videos.

Invitation

From a coloring book or cartoon, find and make a copy of a dalmatian. Enlarge this dalmatian and write in all the party information. Photocopy the invitation and send in red envelopes.

Decorations

- Make a sign for "Kim's Firehouse."
- Set a ladder along the floor, or make one out of crêpe paper streamers to tape along a wall.
- Cut a life-size fire hydrant from poster board, and tape it to a wall or tack it to a tree.
- Arrange coils of garden hose nearby.
- Have a loud bell handy so that you can signal each activity.

Party Starters

Let each child make a badge. Before the party, cut some
self-adhesive labels (at least 3" square) into a badge
shape. Put out washable markers and encourage each arrival to write her name and draw a border of flames. Adhere the badge to the child's clothes or to the plastic
helmet. Take instant photographs of the kids in their
firefighting regalia, sitting at the wheel of a play truck or
car, if possible.

Activities

Firefighters' Training Center

Set up an obstacle course in which kids work together in
pairs or in teams to test their skills. For example, you
might have them race to a pretend "fire" and save a family of teddy bears; some may be hidden. In addition,
they could be asked to help each other climb to a rela-
tively high place to retrieve a stuffed kitten. Time their
efforts with a stopwatch.

Fire and Water

Play the classic red light, green light game (see page
60), using the watchwords "fire" (kids keep moving) or
"water" (kids stop).

Put the Bone on the Dalmatian

In this version of pin the tail on the donkey, blindfolded
guests try to attach the bone closest to the mouth of a big
dalmatian on poster board or foam board. Ask your local
copy shop to enlarge the invitation design as big as pos-

sible, or draw one freehand. Use double-sided tape to adhere brown-paper bones.

Bucket Brigade

Divide the kids into two or more teams of equal number. Supply each child with a paper cup, and each team with two plastic bottles, one full of water and one empty. At the "Ready, Set, Fire!" signal, the first member of each team fills his cup with water from the full bottle. Each team member must pour water into the next person's cup. The last teammate pours the contents of her cup into the empty bottle. Award a prize to the fastest team, and also to those who transported the most water without spilling. If playing indoors, substitute uncooked rice or dried beans for water and a large measuring cup for the second bottle.

Hop to It!

Unless the party is on a warm day, raincoats may be in order for this game! Line everyone up and give each child a cup or a bucket filled with water. Have them race to a finish line, either walking, running, hopping, or jumping. Speed counts less than the amount of water remaining in the racer's cup.

Hose 'Em Down

In this activity, weather permitting, kids use a garden hose for target practice. For the targets, fill plastic cups with water and line them up on a bench or sawhorse. Remind the kids to stand out of the way—firefighters always obey orders.

Food

Fire-Truck Cake

Stack two purchased pound cakes or two homemade loaf cakes, placing ready-to-use or homemade white buttercream frosting in between. Frost the windshield of the truck and then tint the remaining frosting red, yellow, or green (to match your local fire trucks) and use it to frost the truck body. Use more frosting to adhere round, fudge-covered sandwich cookies for wheels, gumdrops for a siren on top, headlights and taillights. Press licorice twists into the cake for fenders and ladders, then use decorator icing in a tube to draw the ladder rungs, outline doors, and fill in any other desired details. You may find dalmatian candles in your local party store to set upon and around the cake, or simply use a squatty candle to set on a building-block house. Only the birthday child can put out this fire!

Flame Quencher-ade

Serve regular lemonade with pink lemonade ice cubes.

Story Time

Fire Cat by Esther H. Averill (Harpercrest). Pickles, a homeless cat, is finally taken in at the firehouse.

Poinsettia and the Firefighters by Felicia Bond (HarperCollins). Poinsettia the Pig is afraid of the dark in her bedroom at night, but takes great comfort in knowing that the firefighters are awake and keeping watch over everyone in town.

Party Favor

When the fire's out, have the kids turn their helmets upside down. Put into them clear bags of any sort of red candy—cinnamon flavored perhaps, but no fireballs!—and a twirly straw, a mini fire truck, or a temporary tattoo of a dalmatian.

Dinosaurs Rule!

Make Mesozoic madness for a fête small tykes will never forget! Never mind that dinosaurs have been extinct for 65 million years. When you're between 4 and 7 years of age, there's no livelier topic. One can feel very brave, knowing there's no real threat of these giant creatures crashing the party! Throw your Jurassic-crazed juvenile a dinosaur party, and watch the fun.

Invitation
Make a T-rex or brontosaurus head that opens its mouth to reveal the party information. Fold construction paper in half and, for each invitation, mark an elongated triangle with its base on the fold. If you wish, add deep zigzags along the sides before cutting out, or cut out using serrated scissors. Draw fierce eyes and nostrils on the top flap; a tongue and teeth, if you need them, inside.

Decorations
- Draw huge dinosaur footprints, well distanced from each other and leading up to your house, with sidewalk chalk. Make one huge pattern so you can trace around it over and over, and let your child color it in.
- Scatter real or plastic ferns around the party zone, along with the biggest rocks you can cart in without getting a hernia.
- Make dinosaur bones: Ask your local fabric store for a couple of cardboard tubes from depleted bolts

of material, or purchase PVC pipe. Use newspaper to wad up four huge balls for each tube, and twist several pages around each cardboard tube to increase its diameter. Cover the balls and tubes with white tissue paper, taping to secure it. Tape two balls at each end of the covered tube or pipe.

- Create cracked-open dinosaur eggs: For each, cover the biggest balloon you can inflate with papier-mâché strips; leave a small opening at one end. When they're dry, use a needle to burst the balloon inside. Using scissors, cut zigzags to enlarge the opening. Be careful to remove all pieces of the broken balloon. Paint the eggs, and draw cracks all around the opening, to indicate that the baby has hatched and is probably wandering around somewhere.

Party Starters

Dino Dig
Beforehand: Bury plastic dinosaurs, some inside plastic eggs, and assorted rocks in a sandbox. Acquire plastic pith helmets.

At the party: Outfit each guest with a pith helmet and set the excavators to work. Limit each guest to one or two trophies so there will be enough for all.

Paleopuzzlerists
Challenge pint-size paleontologists to piece together a dinosaur puzzle. There are many on the market, but you could also enlarge a picture of a dino skeleton and cut it

into odd-shaped pieces. If you wish, use a color photocopy and glue it to thin cardboard before cutting it up.

Activities

Fossil Stepping Stone

Dinosaur footprints aren't essential to the success of
these souvenirs, but if you want to really give the kids a
thrill, carve some dinosaur feet from a foam block or
model them in self-hardening clay, then give them to the
kids to make prints in their plaster of Paris stones.

You need:
- Plastic dinosaurs, pebbles, seashells, fern fronds,
  or other items that can make impressions in wet
  plaster
- Disposable aluminum pie pans
- Cellophane wrap
- Large container of plaster of Paris powder
- Bucket and wood spoon, for mixing and transfer-
  ring plaster
- Wooden craft sticks

1. Let the children choose items for their stepping
   stones; line the pie pans with cellophane.
2. Following the manufacturer's instructions, mix the
   plaster in the bucket, making enough for no more
   than three "stones" in one batch.
3. Spoon the plaster into the pans. Have kids smooth
   the top surface, using a wooden craft stick or the
   like. When the top surface is smooth, kids may begin placing items lightly on the top of the plaster.

4. Within a few minutes, the plaster will start to harden. Kids may now make impressions and, if desired, lift out some elements and perhaps press them in elsewhere. Handprints—or your dino footprints—may be added as well.
5. Let the plaster harden completely. Kids should carry their stepping stones home in the pie pan and remove them from the pan the next day. Stepping stones may be placed in the garden in warm weather but should be brought inside during frost.

T-Rex Tag
Designate one child to be "It"—a roaring T-Rex. Everyone else is a gentle herbivore, grazing in the open. Anyone tagged by T-Rex becomes a T-Rex too, recognized by a ferocious roar and baring of teeth. Continue the game until everyone has been transformed.

Heads and Tails
Designate one child to be the head of a brontosaurus and have everyone else line up behind, each placing his hands on the shoulders of the preceding child. The last child is the tail. Have the head try to catch the tail. If that occurs or if the body breaks apart, change the sequence of children and start the challenge again.

Food

Lunch or Munch
A prehistoric menu could include: Herbivore Hors d'œuvres (raw veggies), Fried Pteranodon (chicken nuggets), Tyrannosaurus Wrecks (salad including dinosaur pasta

shapes), and Fossil Fuels (beverages) with Ice-Age Cubes (ice cubes with gummy dinosaurs frozen inside). Kids will love the puns, so label or announce each item.

Stegosaurus Cake

In addition to your favorite single-layer cake mix and frosting ingredients, you'll need a pastry bag with assorted tips, a dome-shaped snack cake, and some square graham crackers or cookies. To make a base, cover a large cutting board with green cellophane wrap; wrap around the board ends and knot the cellophane on top to form shrubs.

Bake the cake batter in a round 8" or 9" cake pan. Let it cool and remove the cake from the pan. Start by cutting the layer in half, frost one half generously, and top it with the other. Stand this semicircular layer cake on its straight edge in the center of the base.

Tint frosting in your child's preferred pastel color for steg skin (even scientists don't know what color that really was). Frost the cake. For the head, set a dome-shaped snack cake at one end of the cake, and frost that as well. Tint the remaining frosting a darker shade. Using a pastry bag with a large tip, squeeze out generous amounts of frosting to create a tail that curves around on the cutting board; also squeeze out four squatty legs. Change to a finer tip and add spikes to the tail and facial features. One at a time, insert the square graham crackers or cookies diagonally between the cake layers so that half of each cookie is exposed, forming a line of triangles; add frosting if you wish.

Story Time

Can I Have a Stegosaurus, Mom? Can I? Please!? by Lois G. Grambling (Bridgewater Books). Why would anyone want to own a dinosaur? One little boy has all the answers—a dinosaur will protect him from nighttime monsters, will carry the whole class to the museum, will win tug-of-war at camp. The most important reason, however, is that he's found a huge egg; it's cracking and revealing a baby dinosaur inside.

What Happened to Patrick's Dinosaurs? by Carol Carrick (Houghton Mifflin). An imaginary explanation of why dinosaurs became extinct.

Party Favor

There's a ton of dinosaur trinkets out there! Throw a few in the pith helmets: wrapped egg-shaped candies; packs of gummy dinosaurs; capsules that dissolve in warm water to release dinosaur sponge shapes; a dinosaur that grows when you put it in water overnight; a sticky dinosaur on a string; dinosaur tattoos; a pterodactyl glider.

"IT WORKED FOR ME"

"I set aside an area away from the party noises for my tired toddler to take a nap. She was out of the way, and a baby monitor let me know when she awoke—long after the party ended."

SIBLINGS, SWEET SIBLINGS

Face it, siblings are not meant to enjoy someone else getting all the attention. If siblings are much younger or older than the birthday child, but will be attending the party, plan ways they can enjoy the activities too. Throughout this book you'll find suggestions for adapting the activities for children of different ages—often this is as simple as asking older kids to help younger ones.

Here are some ways to keep siblings happily involved.

- Consider providing a jealous brother or sister with a small unbirthday present, or make up a goody bag just for this child and give it to him or her early.

- When you've got heavy-duty sibling rivalry in your family, arrange play dates for everyone but the birthday child.

- Encourage siblings to help: Younger kids can help put out cups and napkins, or hand out the prizes for a game. Older siblings might run a game or two, serve cake, apply temporary tattoos to the guests' arms or legs. Many of the parties in this book contain suggestions for using sibling talents.

- Putting older siblings in charge of the music keeps the rhythm of the party going strong, and the relationship between siblings harmonious. Big brother can choose tapes or CDs ahead of time, change selections, stop the music for freeze tag, and even supply DJ patter.

- If a sibling has a close friend who will absorb her attention, invite that friend to share in (or help at) the party—no gift expected.

- Remind your children often that the day belongs to a specific member of the family, and the rest of them will have the attention and celebration when their birthdays roll around.

Sea Deep

Here's a whale of a good party that's sure to catch kids heart and sole. Kids 4 and over are most seaworthy for this party, but even shrimps, or rather, siblings of 2 and 3, can mussel in on the fun. All activities that follow are landlubbers' specials, guaranteed to keep shy kids from clamming up and aggressive kids from acting shellfish. Of course, this party is even better somewhere that's wetter—a swimming pool, perhaps, if the weather is sea-sonable.

Invitation
Photocopy the party specifics onto blue paper, starting with an enticing line, like "Dive into the Fun!" or "Take the Plunge!" Let the birthday child add stickers of various sea flora and fauna.

Decorations
- Stretch out blue streamers horizontally, for ocean waves.
- Make portholes: Cut tagboard to cover each window. Mark a big circular hole in the center of the tagboard, and draw a rim and screws all around. Cut out the hole and cover it with blue cellophane. Tape the tagboard in the window.
- Purchase floating candles and set them in a large shallow bowl or bucket. Light them for storytime and refreshments, and let the birthday child blow them out before dessert (never leave candles burning).

- If you've got the time and a big appliance box, why not build a submarine? Embellish it with a rotating periscope made from paper tubes. Kids will love getting into it and playing "I spy."

Party Starters
For both of these activities, have an older sibling or another adult on hand to help with gluing.

Fish Heads
You need:
- One piece of paper, 12" × 18"
- Craft foam sheets, 12" × 18", in assorted colors
- Wiggle eyes
- Quick-setting craft glue in little cups
- Cotton swabs
- Assorted trims: sequins, spangles, craft foam shapes
- Paint pens or markers

Beforehand: Make a pattern for the fish head using a sheet of paper the same size as the craft foam sheet. Fold the paper in half lengthwise. From one end (the front) measure 8¼"; on this point center and draft a semicircle with a 3¼" radius. Draw a half-fish shape outside the semicircle, tapering the front for the head, marking a tail at the opposite end, and fins at the sides. Cut out the pattern, unfold it, and, taping it to individual sheets of craft foam, cut out a fish hat for each child. To make the fit adjustable, cut 1"-deep slashes at 2" intervals all around the inner hole. Put out glue in small cups, cotton swabs for applicators, and assorted trims.

At the party: Have each child choose a fish. Check the hole for fit on the child's head, and cut the slashes deeper if necessary. Let the child decorate the fish by gluing on wiggle eyes and trims and adding paint or marker flourishes. Let everything dry for a few minutes before the hats are worn.

PARENTS ALERT

Wiggle eyes and other small trims are choking hazards for kids under 4, so be sure to supervise any small children while they make the fish heads or shell creatures.

   If you hold the party at a pool, make sure there will be a qualified lifeguard on duty and enough adults to supervise every child. Also find out which pool toys and flotation devices are allowed.

Shell Creatures
   You need:
- Assorted seashells
- Small wiggle eyes
- Low-temperature glue gun and glue sticks
- Quick-setting craft glue
- Magnet strips (optional)

Have each child choose one or more shells to make the body, head, and appendages of an imaginary creature. You or another adult can use the glue gun to glue together each design. You can then glue it to another shell, for a base, so that the creature stands erect, or to a magnet strip, so that the creature will hold papers on the refrigerator at home. The kids can glue on wiggle eyes or other small shell details as they wish, using the craft glue.

Activities

Crab Race

Have the kids sit on the ground at the starting line. When you give the signal, they must raise themselves on their hands and feet, and scoot backwards or sideways across a short course.

Crab Soccer

Divide the kids into two teams and have them play a game of soccer—but here's the kick: The kids must assume the same position they took for the crab race and their hands may not touch the ball. Set up two goals, assign one player on each team to be the goalie, and use a lightweight ball.

Flipper Relay

Divide the kids into teams. Have the first player on each team don a pair of flippers. When you give the signal, the outfitted players must run to a goal and back, and then pass their gear to the next player, and so on. Increase the challenge by having each runner carry a bucket of shells without spilling any.

Sea Food

Submarine Sandwich

Fill a large hero loaf with tuna or ingredients you know the kids like. Insert a flexible straw periscope and adhere circular olive slice portholes all around, using a dab of sandwich spread for "glue." Slice up the sub when the kids get to the table.

Deep-Blue Sea Juice

Mix lemonade or apple juice with selzer; add a few drops of blue food coloring.

Octopus Cupcakes

Tint vanilla frosting light blue and use it to frost a cupcake for each child. Center a large gumdrop on each cupcake and set a gummy fish on the edge. Using decorator icing and a star tip, squeeze out two bulging eyes and eight curling tentacles. Using a fine tip, dot the eyes and draw a smile.

Story Time

Swimmy by Leo Lionni (Knopf). A little member of a school of fish realizes there's strength in numbers.

The Rainbow Fish by Marcus Pfister (North South Books). The most beautiful fish in the ocean discovers the value of beauty and friendship.

Party Favor

Cut ocean waves into the top edge of a small blue bag, or draw blue wave lines on a white bag. Insert items such as an octopus, seahorse, or starfish squirter; ocean life fun capsules that expand in warm water; a single-serve packet of goldfish crackers or some gummy fish. Add the child's sea creature.

High Jinks on the High Seas

Yo, ho, ho, and a barrel of fun! Are there adventures to be had and treasures to be found at this pirate jamboree? Aye, matey. Will there be thrills and plundering? Aye, and with parental approval to boot, especially for a Captain Kidd of 4 years or more. And lasses will make fine buccaneers and have a bountiful good time, same as the lads.

Invitation
Draw a map to the party place on white paper, with an X (or skull and crossbones) marking the spot. Photocopy the invitation and "antique" each copy by staining it with a wet tea bag. Let them dry, then tear the edges haphazardly, crumple the invitations, and smooth them out.

Decorations
- Purchase or make Jolly Rogers (pirate flags) to hang: black background with a skull and crossbones.
- Make a ship's steering wheel from a cardboard round such as a pizza or cake base, and attach it over a doorknob where it can be spun.
- Put out a telescope, if you have one, for sighting "other ships to plunder." Or make a toy version by covering a paper towel tube with foil or self-adhesive vinyl.

- Lean oars or paddles against a wall (if you don't own these, borrow some or make stand-ins from foam board).
- Suggest provisions for a long journey at sea: Set out a barrel, a picnic basket, a wood crate, string netting from a big fishing net or hammock, and pillowcases or potato sacks. Have packaged food, clothing, and other necessaries spilling from some of these containers.

Party Starters

Pirate Garb
Begin with an earring made by wrapping a rubber band through a plastic curtain ring and then pulling the loop at one end of the band through the loop at the other end. Hook the rubber band loop over a little pirate ear. Wrap each child's head with a bandanna, top with an eye patch—over the forehead so vision isn't impaired. (All the party stores seem to have eye patches, but if you prefer, cut semicircles from black felt and stitch to them black soft elastic trim.)

Treasure Chests
You need:
- Small lidded containers (such as cardboard jewelry boxes, papier mâché boxes, or cylindrical tins), painted gold
- Quick-setting craft glue
- Assorted trims: acrylic jewels, sequins, spangles, metal washers, star stickers, flat buttons, metallic ribbon

Have each little pirate decorate a box, concentrating on the lid. Let these dry while the party continues.

PARENTS ALERT

Kids love anything sparkling and glittery; supervise toddler mates who might confuse treasure with lunch.

Activities

Walk the Plank

Obtain a 6-foot length of 1" × 6" wood from a lumber-yard or home center to use as a plank. Set the plank on bricks or wood blocks so that it's a few inches off the ground. One at a time, make the pirates walk along the plank, keeping their balance and refraining from falling off. Make this challenge harder by telling the kids to make a U-turn or walk backwards.

Swordplay

You needn't worry about a violent end to this show of prowess. Purchase long pretzel rods or crunchy bread-sticks for the swords. Pair off two pirates, and after everyone yells "En garde!" let them duel. Whoever breaks the other's "sword" goes on to do battle with the next contestant (if both contestants' "swords" break, de-clare a draw and let another pair play). Make the game harder: Let the sword fight take place on the plank de-scribed above. Pirates must keep their balance and win the sword fight in order to meet the next challenger.

Treasure Hunt

Beforehand: Cover a big box with foil and fill this treasure chest with party favors; hide the chest in a closet or other out-of-sight spot. Prepare three maps that give a pictorial hint to finding the chest: Map 1 shows the location of map 2 (with a drawing of your sofa, or a distinctive tree, for instance); map 2 shows the location of map 3, which shows the location of the booty. Hide maps 2 and 3.

At the party: Save this game for the end of the party, when kids can plunder the treasure chest to find their favors. To avoid a free-for-all when they find the chest, set up some rules for divvying up the loot. Hand out map 1, and watch the fun.

Unspinning a Good Yarn

Wrap up a big ball of yarn, binding in trinkets as you go. Give the ball to one little matey, who should unwind it until a trinket falls into her lap, at which point she should pass the ball to the next person, who unwinds until he gets a treat. Naturally there are just enough treasures buried in the ball for one and all. (If the children are old enough, have them wind a new ball as they unwrap the trinkets.)

Food

Treasure Chest Cake

Bake a cake in a loaf pan, or purchase a pound cake with a well-rounded top. Slice off the top to create a "lid," and set it on a sheet of wax paper. The remainder of the cake is the "chest." Spread milk chocolate frosting over all but the bottom surfaces of both pieces. Leaving a 1" margin empty along one long edge, cover the top surface of the "chest" with "treasures": candy necklaces, gold chocolate coins, licorice, gumdrops, jelly beans, and chunks of dried pineapple. To keep the lid propped up, insert a chewy log-shaped candy into each corner of the "chest" opposite the uncovered edge. Use a spatula to lift the lid off the paper, then angle the lid over the chest. Press gummy rings into the sides of the chest, for handles, and onto the center of the lid and chest, for latch hardware. "Stud" the chest and lid with candy dots.

Story Time

Do Pirates Take Baths? by Paul Kennedy (Albert Whitman & Co.). Told in humorous rhyme, this book gives the lowdown on the daily life of pirates, letting kids know, for instance, that "they jump into the sea/ . . . and use sea foam . . . to scrub their knees."

A Pirate's Life for Me by Julie Thompson and Brownie MacIntosh (Charlesbridge). A day aboard a pirate ship.

Party Favor

Let kids plunder the big treasure chest for as many items as will fit into their little treasure chests. Booty might include marbles, fool's gold (rocks), gold chocolate coins and other candies with foil wrapping, parrot pencil toppers, temporary tattoos, jeweled rings, and Halloween skull and crossbones.

"IT WORKED FOR ME"

"We held Gregory's fourth birthday at a gym. There were hoops, mats, balls, bars, swings, and lively music. The kids went nonstop. It was such a success, we did the same party for his fifth birthday!"

GOING ELSEWHERE

Unless your home has a large playroom or finished basement, think about holding the party off the premises. Look around your community. Many facilities have rooms or space you can rent or use at no charge. The range of possibilities stretches from A to Z!

Amusement park   Arcade   Ballet studio

Beach   Bowling alley   Child-care center

Children's play arena   Children's theater

Community center   Craft store   Dance studio

Family restaurant   Farm   Fast-food restaurant

Firehouse   Florist shop

Friend or relative's roomy house

GOING ELSEWHERE

Gym   Miniature golf course   Nature center

Neighbor's swimming pool   Park   Petting zoo

Pizza parlor   Playground   Pottery studio

Recreation center   Skating rink

Slot-car racing center

Woodsy location nearby

Youth group room at a house of worship   Zoo

If you decide on an off-site party location, you should plan the party as thoroughly as if you were holding it at home—you're still the host. If the logistics seem complicated, the key advantages are that opportunities for activities are greatly expanded, and your home stays clean!

Price
Discuss price right up front. See if lessons or demonstrations can be arranged. Some places supply food, a person to run the party, and favors, too. Take these inclusions into consideration, and see if there are various options on party services and supplies. If a friend offers her home or pool, offer to make this a business transaction, suggesting you pay her housekeeper or hire a lifeguard, and clarify which parts of her home the children will be allowed to use.

Schedule

Find out if a reservation is necessary and, if so, how far in advance you must book the facility. Inquire if other parties are likely to be scheduled at the same time. Two groups of kids at a miniature golf course or bowling alley might not be your idea of fun, but could be no problem at a park or zoo.

Facilities

Be sure to check for safety, toilet facilities, and rules and regulations. Be aware of any decorating and cleanup responsibilities that are yours. Always have a first-aid kit with adhesive bandages and antiseptic cream on hand for emergencies.

Arrival/Departure

Decide if you would like kids to be dropped off and picked up at the site or at your home. In any case, it's a good idea to ask for extra parents to chaperone.

Keep It Portable

If your off-premises party is one for which you'll be taking food or supplies to the location, plan accordingly.

- Keep refreshments simple so that a minimum of utensils and paper goods will be needed. Individual juice boxes and nonperishable finger foods will make your life easier.

- Consider a sheet cake you serve from the baking pan. Better yet, bring a plate of brownies or cookies

GOING ELSEWHERE

arranged around a special candle—these won't need plates or forks.

- Organize a cooler and a box for supplies, and be sure to take a box or bag for garbage.

- Keep craft supplies to a minimum, or make them the goody bag so that each child gets his own to use and keep. Pack supplies in a box the right size to hold finished projects.

- Make cleanup part of the fun.

Classroom Parties

Many children enjoy sharing their birthdays with their classmates. Your first responsibility in this situation is to the teacher. Check to see what the school policy is. Knowing that throwing a classroom party is impossible for many parents, teachers often discourage them so as not to wound the self-esteem of children whose parents can't produce a school fête. You may be permitted to bring or send refreshments and have everyone sing "Happy Birthday." If something more elaborate is the norm at your child's school, ask the teacher to help you choose an appropriate activity or a story to read.

"IT WORKED FOR ME"

"I had arranged a party at a petting zoo for Pamela's fourth birthday, but it rained that day. I called everyone and told them to bring boots and umbrellas. It was muddy, but a lot of fun."

Garden Party

Bring on the flower power—it's time to celebrate your perennial's anniversary. Whether held outside in the spring and summer, or indoors to banish winter doldrums or rainy-day blues, this party will be a blooming success for little sprouts 4 years and older. So set the stage for an afternoon of horticultural how-to and watch as even shrinking violets blossom with pride.

Invitation

Fold construction paper in half. Attach a real seed packet with a blob of rubber cement, so that it can be lifted off and used. Write "Jackie is growing up! Come to a birthday garden party!" or "We're planting the seeds for a great party! Hope you can come!"

Decorations

- Simulate a gardening shed: Stack all the flowerpots and materials for filling them. Decoratively arrange the tools, too—a watering can, spade, shovel, trowels, and gardening gloves.
- Glue silk flowers, mini flowerpots, and seed packets to a wreath or a wide-brimmed hat and hang this creation on the front door.
- If you've got a wheelbarrow or can borrow one, it'll make a great prop. Insert silk flowers into any houseplants that aren't in flower (for an outdoor

party, into bushes). Or, use the wheelbarrow as a handy site for the messy planting tasks.

Party Starters

Green-Thumb Flowerpots
You need:
- Terra-cotta flowerpots, 5" diameter
- 4" × 8" sheet of craft foam or a foam innersole
- Disposable plates and plastic wrap
- Acrylic paint in green and a small assortment of other colors
- Paintbrushes
- Jars of water for cleaning brushes
- Packets or pull-up container of moist towelettes, for cleaning hands

Beforehand: Cover a worktable with newspaper. To create a stamp pad, place the foam sheet on a disposable plate, squeeze green paint onto the foam and spread it with a paintbrush, then cover the foam with plastic wrap until ready for use. Pour small amounts of other paint colors into disposable plates and cover these as well.

At the party: Have each child press his thumb onto the stamp pad and apply a green thumbprint to a flowerpot. Suggest various designs to the kids: Thumbprints may be made at random, at regular intervals, or in rows. Or they can be arranged to form a flower, a caterpillar, a bunch of grapes, or hearts. Offer paintbrushes to add details to these designs. Let the paint dry before filling the pots later during the party.

Mini Gardens

Beforehand: Cover the work area with a drop cloth. Choose one or more of the following gardens. Provide a flowerpot, plastic saucer, and tablespoon or plastic scoop for each child. (If you wish, children can use their green-thumb flowerpots; in this case, schedule this activity for later in the party.) Put potting soil into a large baking dish.

At the party: Show the children how to cover the drainage hole in the flowerpot with a shard of pottery or a small rock. Help them fill their pot with one of the following. If you add water, set the pots aside to drain well, otherwise tell the kids to water them when they get home.

- A small annual, such as a marigold, impatiens, or vinca; water these right away.
- Seeds, such as radishes or Kentucky bluegrass, which when planted shallowly will sprout quickly.
- Green floral foam (the kind you can water) and live moss. Have the kids secure the moss to the foam with a couple of hairpins. Give them a choice of decorative elements: some stones, a miniature bird, a little figure, a tiny plastic frog, an artificial butterfly, and a little wood birdhouse are a few possibilities.
- Dry floral foam and Spanish moss, dried flowers with strong, woody stems such as statice or yarrow.

Have the kids secure the moss to the foam with floral u-pins or hairpins and then poke in the flowers.
- A bulb for forcing, such as a paperwhite narcissus, and some pebbles. Instead of providing flowerpots, give each child a clean shallow plastic food tub.

Activities

Flower-Arranging

Beforehand: Stick wire-stemmed artificial flowers into the ground or, in the case of an indoor party, into pieces of foam. Provide a vase or wreath form for each child (or team, if there will be enough children). Make a ribbon prize to award to each arrangement.

At the party: Instruct each child to pick one or more flowers and then insert each in the vase, or wrap it around the wreath.

Clinging Vines

Children become plant life in a new and original line dance, and nobody's a wallflower! You or another adult act as the gardener who directs the action. Play your child's favorite tunes and have everyone try to hold hands throughout.

Choreography might include a grapevine step, where kids move to the left, crossing the right leg over each time, or vice versa. Curling and uncurling their bodies, leaning toward the sun, and vining the line around in figure eights could all be part of the dance moves. Add to the challenge: Ask kids to pass through under the arms of two adjacent people, or through one

or more kids' legs, pulling kids through consecutively
with them.

Smelling Like a Rose

Purchase several fragrant fresh flowers from the florist.
You can find roses, lilies, freesia, and carnations year-
round; stocks and lilacs are available in the spring.
These may, in fact, be the same flowers you use for decorations or for the cake. Set each different type in a separate bud vase or bottle. Let everyone smell them all and
learn their names. Then blindfold the guests, one by one,
and see who can guess what flower is being held under
her nose.

Wheelbarrow Races

Have the kids pair up, with one child walking on his
hands, the other holding the first child's legs off the
ground. See which team can reach the "garden" goal
first, or which team can go for the longest time before
the wheelbarrow collapses.

Food

Flowery Finger Sandwiches

Assemble bread and fillings of choice. Shape the sandwiches with a round, scallop-edge cookie cutter. Press
an apple cutter into, but not all the way through, the
sandwich, leaving an impression of a daisy on top. To
make the flower's center, add a round of cheese, a cherry
tomato half, or a dollop of jelly.

Bouquet Cake

Bake a cake in a bundt pan, the kind with the hole in the middle. Cover a serving plate with a pretty doily. Cool the cake, then remove it from the pan and place it on the plate; insert a slender vase in the hole. Prepare a simple confectioners' sugar glaze, tint it with food coloring if you wish, and pour it over the top of the cake. Dot the surface with edible sugared flowers (available at gourmet shops) or create small blossoms with decorator icing. Using a funnel, carefully fill the vase with water and arrange a bouquet of small pretty flowers in it.

Story Time

The Carrot Seed by Ruth Krauss (HarperCollins). Despite everyone's dire predictions, a boy has faith in the seed he planted.

Planting a Rainbow by Lois Ehlert (Harcourt Brace). A child and her mom plant flowers of every color.

Miss Rumphius by Barbara Cooney (Viking). After fulfilling a lifetime desire to travel, Miss Rumphius yearns to beautify the world in some small way. She decides to plant lupines.

Party Favor

Use a small fruit box or shallow cardboard box—just like those used at a garden shop. Put in the thumbprint pot and/or mini garden, and perhaps a packet of seeds, a plant marker, or some floral stickers.

"IT WORKED FOR ME"

"I always bake a separate cake, with candles, for each of my twin children. We sing the 'Happy Birthday' song twice, once for each child."

CAKE-DECORATING MADE EASY

While the birthday cake is a big deal for children, most kids will be more appreciative of the way a cake looks than of the quality of your baking. Most of the cake ideas in this book can be made from packaged mixes and ready-made frosting, but of course you can use a favorite recipe if you have one. Here are some tricks for creating the special effects.

- If you are going to be cutting a shape or design into the cake, freeze it first. You'll have a nice, firm surface, and you won't tear the cake when you spread the frosting.

- Use a pastry brush or a clean, natural-bristle paint-brush to sweep crumbs away.

- Mark guidelines for cutting by inserting toothpicks an inch apart.

- Use a sharp serrated knife when you cut into or across the cake.

CAKE-DECORATING MADE EASY

- When sculpting or shaping, slice from top to bottom. The edges will stay free of crumbs.

- Use purchased frosting from the can. To create an interesting color, start with vanilla or cream cheese frosting and add food coloring, one drop at a time, mixing until you obtain the color you want.

- Apply frosting with a large spoon, but spread it with a metal spatula. If you will be icing the sides of a cake, do them first, then do the top.

- As you frost the cake, continually dip the spatula into hot water for easier spreading.

- If you need small amounts of several different colors of icing for decoration, use decorator icing in tubes. Also buy a set of tips to screw on the tubes. For large amounts of piped frosting, purchase a pastry bag kit that comes with tips.

- If you're not confident of your drawing ability, use a toothpick to lightly scratch guidelines into the frosting. Follow the lines with decorator icing.

Wild and Wacky Field Day

Neither skill nor strength matters here, everybody's a champ!
Consider throwing this party for your extended family or your
child's entire class. Everyone from 4 to 104 will have a good time.
The games are so silly, or rely so much on dumb luck, that teens
and adults might find themselves on an even playing field with
kids. For safety monitoring, try to have a mature, responsible
"coach," "referee," or "cheerleader" for every four to six youngsters. Assign someone with a camcorder to be the "TV cameraperson," and another who can keep up a patter to be the
"sportscaster."

Invitation

Cut the banner from the sports section of your local paper. Tape it to the top of a sheet of paper on which you've
typed headlines such as "Stacy Turning 7! Wacky Field
Day Celebration to be Held!" and a short news story with
all the details. If you don't have a computer, create the
headlines with letters cut from the newspaper. Photocopy
as many invitations as you need.

Decorations

- Hang colorful banners or flags.
- Post ads for sneakers, sports equipment, and active
  wear around the area.
- Fling old sneakers over doors, tree branches, and
  clotheslines.

- Put paper and crayons on the table, so diners can play games of tic-tac-toe, finger football, or dots.
- Line a plastic baseball or football helmet with cellophane, then fill it with chips, pretzels, and munchies.

Party Starters

Warm-ups
Put out ring toss, a bow with soft foam arrows for archery practice, or a giant ball. Set up a bowling tournament using empty milk cartons as pins and a kickball or soccer ball as a bowling ball. Suggest that kids design an original hopscotch setup with sidewalk chalk.

Outdoor Activities

Leap and Duck
Line up the players in a single file. The action begins with the person at the back of the line, who must alternately leapfrog over the person in front of her, then go through the legs of the person in front of that person, and so on until she reaches the head of the line. The kids in the line will have to alternately squat and stand. The new person at the back repeats the process and the action gets pretty silly. You could clock each person's performance in competition with everyone else, or divide the kids into two teams, and turn this into a relay race.

Tin Can Stilt-Walking
Beforehand: Make a pair or two of stilts; for each, thread nylon clothesline rope through holes

hammered into opposite sides near the bottom
of two empty coffee cans of the same size.

At the party: Turn the cans bottom up and have
the child stand on them, holding the rope reins
to stay on. Clock times to see who can walk
across a course the fastest. (Kids under 4 won't
be able to play this one.)

Water Jumpers

Give everyone a plastic cup filled to the brim with water.
Have the contestants jump from a starting line to a finish
line. The winner is not the speediest jumper but the one
whose cup contains the most water.

Best Hand Forward

This is any standard game played with the left hand by
right-handed kids, and vice versa. Possibilities include
playing catch, batting practice, lawn bowling, and yo-yo
spinning.

Indoor Activities

Long-Distance Shotput

See who can throw a cotton ball or wad of polyester
stuffing the farthest. Expect laughs: These items won't
fly far.

A Lemon of a Relay Race

Divide the kids into teams. Challenge them to push a
lemon with a pencil across the room and carry it back on
a spoon—all without touching the lemon with their
hands (make exceptions for the little kids).

Dining Table Billiards

You'll need at least three people on each of two teams. Mark a dividing line across the middle of the table and position each team around one half of the table. Then see which team can blow a ping-pong ball all the way to the opponents' end. Make it harder by requiring kids to rest their chins on the table while blowing.

Swimmers' Race

Place two children side by side next to a large tub of water in which you've put two feathers of different colors. See which child can blow his featherweight "swimmer" across the tub first.

Shoelace Race

For people who are wearing sneakers, try this one: Have everyone take out the laces completely and then see who is fastest at relacing and tying them. Give wearers of high-tops a head start!

Bizarre Basketball

At each end of a room, have a child stand on a sturdy chair or stool and hold out his arms to form a hoop. Wad up a sheet of newspaper for the ball. Assign three to four kids to each team and have them play a game patterned after regular basketball.

Just for Kicks

Divide the gang into two teams and tell everyone to loosen one shoe and let it dangle on the end of the foot. Set up a laundry basket a few feet away from each team. The object is to fling the shoe off the foot and into the basket (no hands). The team with the most shoes in the basket wins. Try this with kids in a standing position and in a sitting position, but be sure they play one at a time so that they don't clobber each other with flying shoes.

Awards Ceremony

Beforehand: Purchase gold medals or make them: For each, adhere a gold notary sticker to a firm disk. Drill or punch a hole close to the edge and thread through a 1¾-yard length of red, white, and blue striped grosgrain ribbon; knot the ends.

At the party: After the games, kids can watch the videotape, with replays of the funniest moments. Then award everyone a gold medal. If there's time, write a specific claim to fame on the back of each award, such as "Best Egg-Carrier," or "#1 Hopper."

Food

Play Ball Pasta

Gourmet stores often carry macaroni shaped like tennis balls, soccer balls, and the like. Use this to make your child's favorite macaroni and cheese or pasta salad recipe. Great for carbo-loading!

Liquid Energy

Colorful fruit juices, or whatever beverage your child requests.

Fudgy Sports Bars

Bake two boxes of brownie mix in one 8" × 7" or 7" × 9" pan. Frost with vanilla or white chocolate icing tinted bright green. Using white decorator icing and a fine tip, draw the lines of a playing field (baseball diamond, football field, or basketball court, etc.). Position the candles strategically. As you cut the cake into bars, add a decoration to each serving: You'll find hard icing decorations for footballs, helmets, baseballs in a mitt, soccer balls, basketballs in hoops, and more wherever baking goods are sold.

Story Time

Alien Olympics by Stephen Cole and Louise Gardner (Sterling). You won't believe what a "racket" Martians make at tennis, and how high into the sky they can spring!

Clifford's Sports Day by Norman Bridwell (Cartwheel Books). The big red dog is a hit at the neighborhood kids' sports day. As usual, his friends forgive him the havoc his enthusiasm— and big feet—cause.

Party Favor

Use paint pens to write each kid's name on a colorful plastic water bottle. If your budget allows, fill it with lots of little items from the party store or variety store. Look for hockey-stick pencils, baseball cards, jacks and a ball, pickup sticks, small yo-yos, or whistles—sometimes available in sports-related shapes. You'll also find stickers, temporary tattoos, and candy in sporty motifs.

HELP!

Don't try to hold a big party all by yourself. It's exhausting and you might find it challenging to display the necessary joy, enthusiasm, and patience for the kids. Get adults or teenagers to assist you. Try to provide a ratio of one adult to every three children 3 to 4 years old and one adult to every four to five children 5 to 10 years old. Ask the parents of your child's friends if they would be willing to help you, even for part of the time. Offer to reciprocate when their children's parties roll around.

Figure out what you do best, and get help for the things you're not as confident doing yourself. For example, if organizing games is not your thing, find someone who enjoys coaching. If you are all thumbs with crafts, use the ideas you find here but ask a skilled friend to guide kids through the projects.

Paid help need not be expensive. Ask your favorite babysitter, already familiar with your child, to be on hand. A teenager might love the experience of decorating and preparing food and be tolerant of cleanup duties. Or put up a note at a community college—education majors might appreciate the opportunity to see some children in action. Make it clear what tasks and responsibilities you're assigning this young person, and discuss hourly payment up front. Give them only as much responsibility as they're able to handle. Whatever you delegate, keep the children's well-being your own priority.

"IT WORKED FOR ME"

"The best party we ever had featured the owner of our local pet store. She brought a mouse, a lizard, a snake, a parakeet, and a ferret to our home. She told the children about each animal and showed them how to pet it. Her fee was free, because I bought Betas (pretty fighting fish) and mini fish bowls from her store for the party favors."

Backwards B-Day

Kids will convulse into giggles every time they think BACK to this wild and crazy party. This is a totally silly party, hilarious for kids 5 and up. Ask guests to come to the party with their shirts on backwards. As the host, perhaps you'll greet guests in proper attire, too: Wear an apron with the bib in back, the ties in front. The kids will quickly get into the act and contribute lots of backwards ideas.

Invitation
On tracing paper write "COME TO MY BACKWARDS DAY PARTY!" then go over the letters on the reverse side so they're written backwards. Do the same with a clock face, with hands pointing to the time the party will begin. Then, still on the reverse side, write all the important specifics (correctly, not backwards, with the exception of an occasional E or R that's reversed), so no one will be misinformed. Photocopy and send the invitations.

Decorations
- Label the front door EXIT.
- Turn furnishings and accessories around to face the wrong way. Consider anything you can manage: chairs, a small TV, framed photographs on a tabletop, books on a shelf, a welcome mat.
- Hang a HAPPY BIRTHDAY banner (the kind made of cutout letters) wrong side out. Do the

same with any other silhouetted image that would be amusing when reversed.

Party Starters

Give everyone a party favor! Silly Putty would be perfect, because when it's pressed onto the Sunday funnies or other newspaper page, it picks up the image in reverse.

What's My Name?

Pass out painter's caps and tracing paper. Let everyone write his name on tracing paper in big letters, and trace the letters in pencil on the reverse side of the paper. Tape the reversed patterns to the back of the caps. Insert dressmaker's transfer paper in between, and have the kids go over the letters to transfer them; remove the pattern and paper. Let the children go over the letters with acrylic paint pens or fabric paint in applicator-tip bottles (tuck freezer paper behind the fabric to keep the paint from bleeding through).

Activities

Secar Yaler

(That's relay races, backwards!) Divide the kids into teams and have them walk backwards to and from a goal, going as fast as they can.

Worht Gabnaeb

(That's beanbag throw, of course.) Have a contest to see how far each kid can throw a beanbag over his shoulder. No peeking!

Llabtoof

(Do we have to explain?) See how far contestants can kick a football with the heels of their feet.

Seek and Hide

You'll need a large play space for this version of hide and seek, in which one person hides, and everybody looks for her. But anyone who finds the person in hiding joins her. If a finder thinks other kids are watching when he makes the discovery, he should pretend not to see anything and come back later. At the end, everyone is crowded into one hiding place, and the last person must find them all.

Backwards T-Ball

If you've got the space for a small baseball diamond, reverse some of the traditional patterns of movement: Have a batter run backwards to third base, then to second base, then to first base, then home. Keep score in minuses rather than pluses.

Food

Plan an extremely light meal, because kids are going to start with dessert, and probably won't require anything after. Why not make an upside-down cake? Place all the candles in the middle, and cut slices around them. Let everyone eat their serving, then light the candles and let the birthday child blow them out.

Story Time

> **The Stupids Have a Ball** by Harry Allard and
> James Marshall (Houghton Mifflin). Kids hoot

over the backwards way this family does everything.

The Topsy Turvies by Francesca Simon (Dial Books). The Topsy Turvies start their day at midnight, wear pajamas outdoors, and serve tomatoes for dessert after the cake.

Grand Finale

Have each child don his painter's cap so the name is at the back of his head. Take an instant photograph of the back of each child's head. Frame it in a picture mat upon which you've written the child's name, backwards of course. Kids will go into hysterics every time they look at it.

HIRING ENTERTAINMENT

For talent, ask your friends for recommendations. If that doesn't prove fruitful, call the local high school guidance counselor or college drama department for suggestions. Most schools have a job board where you could post a help-wanted advertisement for free. Sometimes local entertainers advertise in the yellow pages, the classified section of the newspaper, or on bulletin boards in such places as the town library or corner store.

Here are some types of entertainers you might find:

- A college-age drama major who can do funny voices for story-time selections
- An amateur or professional magician
- A clown

```
┌─────────────────────────────────────────────┐
│              HIRING ENTERTAINMENT             │
├─────────────────────────────────────────────┤
```

- Someone from the local comedy club who has a way with youngsters
- A talented artist who can do face painting
- A musician who invites kids to sing along
- A puppeteer
- A professional storyteller
- Someone who can make things with balloons
- A ceramic artist or potter who can make tiles with the kids
- An art teacher
- A dance instructor
- A lifeguard
- A juggler
- A mime

Check Them Out

Interview anyone you don't know ahead of time. Find out how long the entertainer has been doing children's parties, how long the show or activity will last, what supplies you or the entertainer will provide, and how much it will cost. If the entertainer has a video, watch it. Ask for references and *call them*.

Time It Right

If you've hired help to provide entertainment, realize that 15 minutes for the playpen set, 30 minutes for little ones 3 to 5, and 45 minutes for kids 6 and above are plenty.

Space Cadets

5 . . . 4 . . . 3 . . . 2 . . . 1 . . . **blast off for fun!** Future astronauts, particularly those now ages 5 to 8, will love you for launching this party. Here are plenty of activities to keep high spirits in orbit. To further expand the universe, arrange a visit to a planetarium or observatory, or send a model rocket into outer space—you can depend on the kids to provide a countdown, loud and clear.

Invitation

"One small step for Joey, one giant bunch of fun for everyone!" Print a similar headline and the party specifics on paper. Your home computer may have a space-age font and clip art for this. If not, photocopy the invitation onto stationery with a space theme, or embellish it with stars and other stickers. If your child can do it, show him how to fold each invitation into a streamlined paper space shuttle.

Decorations

- Look in a crafts store for wood or foam stars, crescents, rings, and balls in assorted sizes; hang them from the rafters, curtain rods, ceiling lights, and doorways.
- Use a black tablecloth (often found with the over-40 party notions) that you've decorated all over with silver sticky stars.
- Put up a poster of a satellite view of the earth.

- Assemble a life-size astronaut mannequin: Stuff white clothing with wads of newspaper or polyester stuffing. Cover gloves and boots with aluminum foil. For a head, tape clear plastic over the opening of a bike helmet and set it on top.

Party Favor

Flying Spaceships
You need:
- Disposable foam or paper plates, cups, bowls
- Plastic drinking straws
- Stickers: circles, stars, and patriotic themes
- Colored PVC tape
- Quick-setting craft glue
- Permanent-ink markers, crayons
- String

Let the little rocket scientists create their own intergalactic transports. Suggest using a disposable plate as a base to fuel a spinning spaceship with flying power, or using string to pull a vertical rocket—mechanically minded kids might even show you how to set up a string pulley system.

Activities

Spaceship Launch
Let kids send their spaceships on voyages across the room or backyard. Make sure the glue is dry first!

Farthest Flight

Given a lot of outdoor space, pass out Frisbees so that kids can send these flying saucers sailing in competition. Set up a relay race where each team must throw a Frisbee from space station (kid) to space station (kid) to reach a distant star—that is, a tree or other landmark.

Saturn Ring-Toss

Set balls of different sizes all over a playing area. Have the kids try to toss hula hoops or smaller rings made with cardboard strips over the planets—do you think those celestial orbs will hold still when grazed by a flying ring?

Moons of Jupiter

Have the kids stand in a circle, facing out, and have them toss a series of ping-pong balls, small rubber balls, tennis balls, kick balls, and even beach balls around in an "orbit." (But be fair, don't ask the kids to play with more balls than there are players.) Declare dropped balls "lost in space" (out of play). If there are enough guests, set up two circles and see which can keep the most balls going for a fixed amount of time.

Watch Out for Asteroids!

Play a space-age version of dodge ball using a soft, high-bounce ball.

Food

Moon Cake

Bake a two-layer cake. Tint vanilla or cream cheese frosting a bright yellow-green and fill and cover the cake. Let the frosting harden for just a few minutes, then gently press the outside of a melon baller into the surface of the cake to create crater holes. Add a plastic figure of an astronaut or a spaceship, and an American flag pick. Serve with space dots ice cream—advertise it as the ice cream of the future—which you'll find at push-cart vendors at malls and movie theaters.

Story Time

My Brother Is from Outer Space by Vivian Ostrow (Albert Whitman & Co.). A young boy, convinced that his brother is an alien, offers proof by compiling a book of evidence. Readers will laugh along with the narrator's parents, who reassure the boy that, though the brother is indeed a character, he's definitely human.

My Place in Space by Robin and Sally Hirst (Orchard Books). An Australian boy tells the bus driver exactly where he lives. Close inspection of the pictures reveals alien shenanigans.

Party Favor

Use a darning needle to poke constellation-like holes in small black bags. Put a small flashlight, some space-age sweets (small candy bars with planetary names or packets of colorful fizzing candies), plus a small plastic robot, space-ball shooter, moon ball, or lunar crystals (stretchable putty with glow-in-the-dark sparkles) inside each. Tell the kids to shine the flashlights inside the bags to see the portable night sky.

"IT WORKED FOR ME"

"I always tell kids 'One last turn for everyone!' or 'Two-minute warning!' so that an activity doesn't end too abruptly."

¡Fiesta!

Olé! Viva México! Draw upon the hot colors, rich flavors, and Spanish, Latino, and indigenous cultures of our most exotic American neighbor. Children 5 and over will most appreciate this chance to take a make-believe trip south of the border.

Invitation

To make a folk-framed announcement, first write the party specifics on paper, filling a space about 2" smaller in each direction than the envelope dimensions; include some simple graphics such as a sun, sombrero, or flowers, if you like. Photocopy this as necessary, cut them out, and have your child add some color. For each invitation, cut a piece of heavy aluminum foil to a size slightly smaller than the envelope. Glue each invitation to a piece of foil and scallop the edges. Use a hole punch to make holes all around and a nail to pierce finer holes and inscribe a zigzag or wavy line.

Decorations

- Hang "papel picado" (meaning pierced paper) banners across the ceiling, doorway, or between any high places. Make accordion folds across brightly colored sheets of tissue paper, then cut little geometric shapes along the folded edges: triangles, squares, circles, rectangles, hearts. Add little circles with a hole punch. Unfold the paper and tape one short edge over a long length of string. Tie the ends of the string across the party area.

- Make hot-colored flowers from large sheets of crêpe paper or tissue paper, and tape them everywhere.
- Drape bright-colored or striped blankets over furniture; spread your brightest bed sheet or fabric yardage over the table.
- Hang a couple of sombreros on walls or doors.
- Line up pots of red geraniums in a window or across the party table.

Activities

Bullfights

First provide some simple costumes. For the bull, attach cardboard horns to a headband for one child to wear, and tuck a "tail"—a crêpe-paper streamer—into the child's waistband at the back. Use a yard of red fabric for the matador's cape. To play, the matador entices the bull to charge at his cape, and tries to pull the tail off the bull; the bull tries to take the cape, which the matator tries to retain. The kids can take turns. Those not playing should stand in a ring around the players and give appropriate yells and whistles.

Mexican Jumping Beans

Tie each child's legs together at the ankles with grosgrain ribbon or a bandanna. Have the kids jump across a course in a race or relay race.

Hurrying to Market

In many cultures where cars are luxuries, people are skilled enough to carry their wares to market in baskets on their heads. Challenge kids to balance light loads on their heads, without using their hands. Make it easier by supplying rings of braided plastic dry-cleaner bags, which create a stable base for the basket (you can use paper or plastic bowls instead of baskets). Stage a competition based on distance or speed.

Mexican Hat Dance

You probably know this old standard. Instruct the kids to fold their arms across their chests or place hands on hips, then kick forward one leg at a time to the beat of the traditional Mexican Hat Dance. When the tempo changes, demonstrate how to link arms with a partner and circle around the room. If you don't have the appropriate music, use any song that changes tempo, or let the kids dance to their own beat. Once they start, they won't want to stop!

Food

Tortilla Chips

You'll need a big bowl of these! Choose different colors and flavors. The children will be interested to know that corn is a very ancient grain native to the Americas; it was cultivated for centuries before the Europeans came here.

Quesadillas

These are the Mexican answer to grilled cheese sand-wiches. Lay slices of American or grated Monterey Jack cheese between soft tortillas on a plate; cover with wax paper. Microwave on high for one minute or until the cheese melts. Take out, cut into wedges, and serve.

Make Your Own Tacos

Follow the directions on taco kits from the supermarket, but use the seasoning packet at half strength so that the meat filling is less spicy. Put out shredded lettuce, juli-enned jicama (a crispy root vegetable), grated cheddar or Monterey Jack cheese, chopped tomatoes, sour cream, chopped black olives, and taco sauce and have the kids choose their own fillings.

Cactus Fruit

Carve a hole in the side of a small watermelon. Scoop out the fruit and cut it into chunks. Set the melon shell upright on a big terra-cotta flowerpot. Fill it with water-melon chunks and other pieces of fruit. Stick toothpicks into the melon to simulate cactus spikes.

Churros

The Mexican cousin to the doughnut, these pastry sticks can be laid out on a tray so that they spell out the birth-day child's name. Serve them with a fruity flavor of sherbet. Let the birthday child blow out colorful fat candles in a variety of bright, Mexicali colors. The recipe makes 12 churros; make as many batches as you need.

You need:
- 1 cup sifted flour
- 1 teaspoon salt
- 1 egg
- Oil for deep frying
- 1 slice bread
- ½ lemon, cut in wedges
- Confectioners' sugar

Sift flour and salt into a mixing bowl. Make a well in the center of the flour and pour in 1 cup of boiling water. Beat with a whisk until the mixture is fluffy and smooth. Add the egg and keep beating until the batter is smooth and shiny.

Pour 3" to 4" oil into a deep pot, and heat to 375°F on a thermometer. Flavor the oil by immersing a slice of bread and wedges of lemon; remove them as soon as the bread turns a dark brown.

Pour some batter into a pastry tube with a star tip. Squeeze 3" to 5" snakes of batter into the hot, flavored oil. When the churros are a golden color, remove them with tongs and let them drain on paper towels. Roll them in confectioners' sugar while hot.

Story Time

Fiesta by Ginger Foglesong Guy (William Morrow). While this party rocks, kids will be counting in English and Spanish.

Going Home by Eve Bunting (Harper Trophy). Mexican immigrants return to their mother country for the holidays.

Party Favor

The burro piñatas!

DOLLAR-SAVING TIPS

Of course you want your child's party to go down in history as the best ever, but there's no reason to go broke producing it. Here are some ways to cut costs.

- Visit the party-goods store before you nail down your theme. You'll see what's available and affordable.

- Make the invitations yourself. Produce multiples with a black and white photocopier, and have your child color them in. Fold invitations into thirds to make a self-mailer. Save on postage by delivering the invitations personally.

- Make the food yourself rather than buying it. Or, buy plain, frosted cake or cupcakes and add the decorations yourself. Look through your child's bins of plastic figures; you're sure to find some items that fit your theme. Just clean them off and set them down on the cake.

- Make use of mail-order companies to purchase trinkets by the dozen two or three weeks in advance—it will almost always save you money. Decorations, costumes, party ware, and goody bags and their contents may all be requested by phone. One popu-

DOLLAR-SAVING TIPS

lar choice, Oriental Trading Co., at (800) 228-2269, just started putting out a special birthday party catalog in addition to their regular, seasonal catalog of gadgets, gimmicks, and gewgaws.

- Visit dollar stores, variety stores, and discount department stores for supplies.

- Create your own play clay. Little children will love squishing it through their hands. (See the Pizzeria party on page 189). Here's the recipe:

> 1 cup flour
> 1 cup water
> ½ cup salt
> 2 teaspoons cream of tartar
> 2 tablespoons vegetable oil

Mix these ingredients in a pot and cook them over medium heat until the mixture is firm. Knead the dough until the consistency is smooth. Divide it into individual portions, color each portion with different food coloring, and wrap tightly in plastic wrap. Store it in the refrigerator.

Beach Bonanza

Have all the fun of a day in the sun—with no sand in kids' eyes!
Bring the beach to you, rain or shine. Make a big splash for 5-to
8-year-old gulls and buoys . . . for shore! If the weather is warm,
suggest guests come in bathing suits, flip-flops, and cover-ups.

Invitation

Write the party information on a piece of paper folded to
fit inside a scallop shell (you can purchase these as baking shells from gourmet shops); tape the paper into the
shell. Deliver by hand or mail in a padded envelope. Or,
use rubber stamps of shells to create your own invitations—your child will enjoy helping.

Decorations

- Cover the table with brown paper to look like sand.
  Make a sand castle centerpiece from small corru-
  gated cardboard boxes and rolled-up sandpaper
  "turrets." Scatter some seashells around.
- Bring in some picnic coolers.
- Set up a beach umbrella and beach chairs.
- Drape beach towels around.
- Blow up a few beach balls.

Party Starters

Beach Shades

Give everyone a pair of plastic sunglasses. Set out
squeeze bottles of craft glue, plus an assortment of embellishments: sequins, spangles, buttons, ribbon roses,
colorful pipe cleaners, tiny seashells, and craft foam
shapes. If there are younger guests, supervise them
while they choose the decorations, and have an older
child or an adult glue the pieces together.

PARENTS ALERT

Children 2 and under should not be given sunglasses. Give
them sunshades instead.

Sand Art

You need:

- Bags or jars of colored sand (available at craft
  stores and pet stores)
- Small, clear-glass baby food or jelly jars, one per
  child
- Plastic spoons
- Cone-shaped paper drinking cups, with the tips
  pierced or snipped off to make funnels
- For older kids: 22-gauge stub wire (available at
  craft stores)
- Quick-setting craft glue

Beforehand: Cover the table or floor with newspaper. Open the bags or jars of sand. Or, do this outdoors, weather permitting.

At the party: When the kids arrive, give each a paper cone, spoon, and jar. Explain the following process to those unfamiliar with it:

1. Place the paper funnel with its hole inside the jar. Spoon some sand into the funnel, letting it run into the jar until it covers the bottom. Repeat to add a second color of sand.
2. Continue to add sand until the jar is filled. Use two colors for a pattern of stripes, or several colors to make a rainbow. When the jar is full, older kids can push stub wire into the sand along the sides of the jar to create a design of arches and scallops.
3. Have the child use his finger to spread a little glue all around the inside rim of the jar lid and then screw on the lid.

Activities

Beach Blanket Bingo

Make your own playing boards and set out baskets of small shells or pebbles for kids to use as markers.

Volleyball

For an out-of-doors party, use a beach ball. If the party must be indoors, use a balloon, tie string between two chairs for a net, and confine all players to their knees.

Beach Ball Bull's-Eye

Set up an obstacle course through which beach balls must be thrown. Suspend hula hoops with string along the way. To make the game harder, have the kids kick the ball.

Frisbee games, kite-flying, limbo, and sand-castle building in a sandbox will all make your guests feel as if they've been to the seashore!

Food

Starfish and Sand-Dollar Sandwiches

Make your child's favorites, then cut them out with a star or circle cookie cutter. Serve on a platter covered with shredded lettuce or spinach "seaweed."

Bucket of Sand

First, pulverize enough vanilla wafer cookies to produce 2 cups of cookie crumbs, and set aside. Combine 2 packages of vanilla instant pudding-and-pie-filling mix with 4 cups of milk, following the package directions. Use a rubber scraper to fold in 8 ounces of nondairy whipped topping, and then the contents of one 10½-ounce box of miniature chocolate chip cookies. Spoon half of this mixture into a clean 2½-quart plastic beach bucket. Sprinkle with half the cookie crumbs, then repeat the layers. Cover and chill at least 4 hours. Decorate with seashell-shaped chocolates and pebble candies. Use a brand-new sand shovel to serve the cake.

PARENTS ALERT

Omit the pebble candies if children under 5 will be attending the party.

Story Time

At the Beach by Anne F. Rockwell (Aladdin Paperbacks). A vicarious trip for the playpen set.

Pigs on a Blanket by Amy Axelrod (Aladdin Paperbacks). Fun with math and time and pigs.

The Bears' Vacation by Stan and Jan Berenstain (Random House). Papa Bear teaches beach safety by poor example.

Party Favor

Give your party-goers plastic water bottles or plastic buckets with their names written on in paint pen. Some salt-water taffy would be beachy-keen!

"IT WORKED FOR ME"

"To make choosing teams for games fair and easy, I color the ends of ice-cream sticks and place them, color-end down, in a can. Each child picks a stick, and those with matching colors are on the same team. No more tears or fights—what a relief!"

Puppet Show

Make a puppet! Put on a puppet show! Recommended for children 5 years of age on up, the script for this party is fairly loose and filled with quick-and-easy possibilities. Depending on the attention span, amount of time, number of kids, and the birthday child's desires, kids can make stick puppets, hand puppets, or both, as so many of the materials are the same.

Invitation

Transform the backs of 5" × 7" clasp envelopes into sack puppets, including a balloon quote announcing the big event. Write "Casting Call for Ryan's Puppet Show Birthday Party" and all the party information on a separate sheet of paper, asking guests to bring a knock-knock joke for a show and inviting them to bring their own puppet to add to the cast, if they wish. Photocopy this and insert one into each envelope.

Decorations

- Use lots of colorful paper goods and hang crêpe paper streamers to create an old-world Punch and Judy effect.
- Make individual puppet theaters and set them at each place at the table: Use empty, single-serve cereal boxes; remove the tops (the bottom of the theater) and cut open the perforated flaps on the front to create shutter-like "curtains." Spray-paint the

boxes with brilliant hues. The kids will use these
with the stick puppets they make.

• Set up a kid-size puppet theater: Select a doorway
to a room you won't be needing. Put a tension rod
across it about 3 feet above the floor, and another
tension rod near the top. Drape a length of fabric
over the lower rod to make the stage front; decorate it with crêpe paper streamers or other embellishments. Rig stage curtains with fabric and
clip-on curtain rings and hang them from the upper tension rod. At show time, kids can hide behind the lower drape as they raise their puppets
over it to perform.

Party Starters

Sock Hand Puppets and Stick Puppets
You need:
• Clean socks
• Pink poster board, cut into 2½" × 4" ovals for
  mouths
• Large wood craft sticks (tongue depressors)
• Quick-setting glue in squeeze bottles
• Low-temperature glue gun and glue sticks (optional)
• Assorted embellishments in large scale for sock
  puppets, small scale for stick puppets: wiggle eyes;
  pom-poms; felt—some scraps, but lots of precut
  shapes for tongues, lips, cheeks, animal ears,
  spots; strands of yarn; ribbon bows; ribbon roses;
  mini hats; pipe cleaners; spangles; washable markers; fabric markers.

Beforehand: Make up an example of each type of puppet, so that kids have some reference and inspiration. Enlist a teenager or older sibling to help at party time, especially if there will be any toddler puppeteers who will require supervision around the small pieces. If you wish, you can give the sock puppets mouths before the party, or wait and do this with the children: Fold a poster-board oval in half widthwise, and glue it to the instep area of the sock, halfway between the toe and heel areas. If you're doing this at the party, use a low-temperature glue gun so that kids can immediately add other features.

At the party: Let kids assemble their puppets. The array of items for embellishments will provide the kids with plenty of ideas, but you might make suggestions, such as gluing a wiggle eye to a large pom-pom for a bulging eye; gluing on oversize pom-pom nose to achieve a goofy look; using markers or felt to dress a stick puppet; styling hair with yarn in an unexpected color. Set the creations aside for about 15 minutes to allow the glue to set. Meanwhile, occupy the kids with a story or other activity.

Activities

Gepetto and Pinocchio

Put the kids into pairs, and let each pair decide who will be the puppet and who the puppet master. Set each team a simple task, such as crossing the room and picking up a block. Explain that puppets can't move on their own—

before each movement can be made, the puppet master must tap the puppet's appropriate leg, foot, arm, and so on—so this game takes more thought than players might expect. When the mission has been accomplished, have the kids switch roles and maybe partners, too.

Showtime!

Keep the kids in the same or different pairs and ask each pair to put on a short act for the group, using the knock-knock jokes they brought, or others you supply. Have the performers go behind the puppet theater and arrange everyone else in front. Some kids will need prompting, but anything goes and each "act" lasts only about a minute.

Puppet Tag

Have each child don a sock puppet or other hand puppet from home and play tag! The twist? One puppet is "It" and may tag only other puppets.

Food

Cookies-on-a-Stick Puppets

Use 5" people or animal cookie cutters to shape these. For 1 dozen cookies, purchase 1 package of refrigerated sugar cookie dough, 12 wooden craft sticks (tongue depressors), assorted colored sugars, and small candy decorations. Preheat the oven to 350°F; grease cookie sheets. Roll out half the dough to ¼" thickness, cut out cookies, and place them on a cookie sheet; repeat with the remaining dough. Press a stick into the bottom of each cookie, making sure the stick is well embedded, and smooth some dough over it. Carefully turn the cookies with a spatula so that the sticks are underneath. Sprinkle colored sugar on top. Bake for about 7 minutes or until the edges are just lightly browned. Cool on the cookie sheets for 2 minutes, then on wire racks for 20 minutes. Add features or other embellishments with decorator icing fitted with a writing tip, if you wish.

To serve, arrange the cookies on a platter around a brick or bowl of ice cream. Put birthday candles in the ice cream.

Story Time
The Funny-Paper Puppet Caper by Bonnie West (Carolrhoda Books). A mystery that starts with a puppet folded from newspaper.

Walt Disney's Pinocchio by Gina Ingoglia (Disney Press). This marionette is pretty special.

Party Favor
Give each child a small gift bag in which to put her cereal-box puppet theater and the puppet she made. Add a small book about using your hands as shadow puppets—look in bookstores, museum stores, or the activity book section of your local toy store. You could also include a small flashlight.

Rain Forest

The rain forest makes a hot topic for an exotic party. You can celebrate the glory of a rain forest come rain or come shine, right at home. Use recycled items whenever possible—after all, the lesson of the rain forest is that we must protect the earth's resources. Children 5 and up will enjoy both the lesson and the party.

Invitation

Party stores sell plastic or rubber frogs—many patterned after the poison dart variety found only in the rain forest. Purchase one frog for each guest you will invite. Write all the party particulars on a sheet of paper, starting with "Hop on over to a rain forest party in honor of Jamie's birthday." Photocopy this sheet, and wrap up each frog in an invitation. Tie the packet closed with twine or raffia, and insert a leaf. If you can't hand-deliver these packets, mail them in small padded envelopes.

Decorations

- Hang ropes (the twisted paper variety is fine) in a tangle on high—from the ceiling or between trees in the backyard. Add crêpe-paper leaves taped along these "vines."
- Put out stuffed animals, some swinging through the vines.

- Buy or borrow from the library a tape of rain-forest sounds: animal noises and of course lots of rain showers and rainstorms.

Party Starters

Bird of Paradise Plant Stick
You need:
- Recycled rag-content watercolor paper
- Scissors
- Permanent ink markers
- Hole punch
- Pictures of parrots and other exotic birds
- Watercolor paints and water
- Broad foam paintbrushes and small paintbrushes
- 12"-long stick or dowel, for each
- Paper fasteners
- Bright feathers (available at craft stores)
- Masking tape and quick-setting craft glue

Beforehand: On a sheet of 8½" × 11" paper, draw a bird body and wing shape. Using these as patterns, cut out one of each shape from watercolor paper for each child. Mark the beak and eye, using a permanent marker. Use the hole punch to pierce each body and wing. Put out the rest of the supplies.

At the party: Show kids the bird pictures. Explain the following process to them and help them put their birds together. They can play "Nuts, I Missed," following, while the paint dries.

1. Tell the kids to first brush some "rainwater" on their shapes, using a broad foam brush. Then encourage them to paint their birds any way they like. Let the paint dry for a few minutes.
2. Instruct the kids to attach the wing to the body with a paper fastener, and then tape a dowel or stick to the back. They can glue feathers to the ends of the wing, the tail, and the crest of the head.

Nuts, I Missed!

Put out shallow plastic bowls. Have the kids toss nuts, still in their shells, toward the bowls. See who can get the most nuts into the bowls or into one particular bowl.

PARENTS ALERT

Omit peanuts from this game and don't put out nutcrackers—this will save you from worrying about any nut allergies guests might have.

Activities

Rain-Forest Animal Charades

Whisper the name of an animal that lives in the rain forest into the ear of a guest. This guest must act like the animal while others guess her identity. Here are some possibilities: frog, toucan, parrot, leopard, tiger, chimpanzee, gorilla, lizard, snake, butterfly, tarantula.

Classic Animal Games

Either of these will be a success: monkey-in-the-middle or leap frog. And, of course, parroting (repeating a phrase whispered all around a circle, and seeing what finally comes back to the initiating player—usually known as telephone).

Food

Fern-Print Ice Cream Cake

Using two boxes of mix, bake brownies in two round cake pans. Let them cool and remove the brownies. Place slightly softened mint chocolate chip ice cream between the layers. Spread jelly around the sides, then press shredded coconut (or cookie crumbs) into the jelly. To decorate the cake, place a couple of leather-leaf fern fronds from the florist shop on top of the cake, and dust it with confectioners' sugar. Remove the ferns carefully, lifting them straight up off the cake to leave a reverse stencil. Keep the cake in the freezer until 30 minutes before serving, then transfer to the refrigerator.

Story Time

   A Jaguar in the Rain Forest by Joanne Ryder (William Morrow). The reader is the jaguar.

Party Favor

Give each child his very own tree: a small tree seedling. If he or she has no yard, there are probably places nearby that can provide the tree with a home. Whip up a quick burlap sack for each seedling, or place it in a brown paper bag.

Detective Story

Who done it? You'll be glad you did! Kids of any age will qualify as "Most Wanted," but with clues to untangle and mysteries to solve, this party is best for children who can read—at least a little. Try to assign one good reader to each detective "squad" and call upon other junior sleuths for puzzle assembly, speed, and creativity.

Invitation

Cut letters and words from newspapers and magazines and glue together a fake ransom note that says "Guess who's having a mystery birthday party?" or "Top secret: How much fun we're going to have at Fran's birthday party." Add the party particulars and make photocopies. Mail each invitation in an envelope marked CONFIDENTIAL.

Decorations

- Trace the heel and toe of a man's shoe and cut out black construction-paper shoe prints to tape all over the party area—even the walls!
- Add cutouts of giant magnifying glasses and question marks to the walls.
- Tack mazes, riddles, or word searches all around.

Party Starters

Most-Wanted Posters

One at a time, costume each child in a rumpled raincoat and fedora, take an instant-photo mug shot, and glue it to a 5" × 7" sheet of illustration paper. Have the child add his fingerprints (use a black washable-ink stamp pad) below the photo. Write the child's name on the poster.

Fingerprint Fugitives

Let the kids make several fingerprints, then use fine-tipped markers or colored pencils to turn the fingerprints into creature criminals for little wanted posters: Robber Rat; Snatcher the Snake; Lyon the Lion; Sneaky Pete, the Parakeet. Encourage kids to come up with their own fugitives.

Disguise Dese Guys

Put out some fun disguises: pairs of glasses or sunglasses, one oversize, one with a big nose and mustache; washable face makeup; a wig; a kerchief; funny hats; an eye patch; a self-adhesive mustache and beard. Let kids try on some different looks.

Activities

Solve the Crime

Somebody has stolen the goody bag loot and hidden it away, along with several clues. Read the directions through ahead of time to see what to do before the party.

1. Divide the kids into two or three detective "squads," with three to five people on a team. As-

sign each squad a color. Each team must find clues keyed to their team color. Give each squad a detective kit with a washable marker, a pad and pencil, and the first clue.

2. Put colored tape or stickers on envelopes, so that each squad must locate its own appropriately colored clues. Hide the clues in these envelopes all over the designated playing area, choosing the largest outside or indoor party space possible. You may wish to hide envelopes under flowerpots, in shoe boxes, in the mailbox, under furniture, or behind curtains. While the squads need not be competitive with each other, it's more fun if each squad is secretive about finding its clues only.

3. Give each team three clues telling them where to look for something, for example: "Look under a big flat thing," and have the envelope taped to the underside of a table, or "Look where the sun shines in," and put the envelope alongside the windowsill. Try to have the teams move in different directions, a different order, or a different area to keep the challenge exciting for everyone.

4. For extra fun, you can create clues that must also be decoded. Here are some ideas:
   - Write the clue and then cut it into puzzle pieces that must be assembled in order for the clue to be read.
   - Write the clue in white crayon on white paper; the children will have to coat the paper with washable marker to reveal the crayon clue.
   - Substitute a number from 1 to 26 for each letter

of the clue (with 1 standing for A, 2 for B, 3 for C, etc.).

5. The last clue leads to a construction paper key, which must be handed in to the host parent. When all keys have been retrieved, the goody bag loot is allotted. Perhaps it is inside a box wrapped in blue paper, which is inside a bigger box wrapped in red paper, which is inside a box wrapped in yellow paper. Only the same-color key will allow a box to be opened.

What's Missing?

Each kid gazes for 10 seconds at a tray full of small objects, such as a ball, spoon, small cup, key, paper clip, ring, seashell, scoop, bolt, and eraser. While the first player closes her eyes, another guest removes one object. The player must guess what's missing.

Secret Messages

Let kids draw or write on sheets of white paper using a cotton swab dipped in lemon juice. When dry, the markings will be visible only when the paper is held up to the light. Another variation: Let them use glow-in-the-dark paint on white paper. The messages will appear in a dark room!

Food

Phony-Baloney Sandwiches

Spread deli meat on long Italian bread and cut the sandwich into small slices.

Secret Message Salad

Combine alphabet pasta with slices of celery; carrots; drained, canned corn kernels; and ranch dressing—let the kids hunt for words as they eat.

Hidden Surprise Drink

Drop a maraschino cherry with a stem into each compartment of two ice cube trays. Fill one tray with cranberry-raspberry juice, another with orange or mango juice, then freeze. Drop some ice cubes into clear glasses and fill with a mixture of the remaining fruit juices and ginger ale.

PARENTS ALERT
Slice cherries in half lengthwise before freezing for kids 3 and under.

Master Sleuth Birthday Cake

Prepare two brownie mixes in one bowl, and divide the batter into one 15" × 10" jelly-roll pan and one 8" round cake pan. Bake according to package directions, testing for doneness separately; then cool and remove from pans. Place the rectangular brownie on a serving platter and frost the top with vanilla icing. Then, to create the magnifying glass, place the round brownie off-center on top of the rectangular one; frost the top. For the magnifying glass handle, set a single-serve chocolate-covered creme-filled devil's food cake roll between the magnifying glass and one corner of the rectangular brownie. Use decorator icing to write "Happy Birthday" atop the cake: Within the magnifying glass, make the letters twice as large as elsewhere. For a handprint, lay your child's hand on a fruit snack which has not yet been peeled from the plastic. Trace around the hand with a skewer, and cut out the handprint with scissors.

Story Time

Nate the Great by Marjorie Weinman Sharmat (Young Yearling). A series of short mystery books starring a junior Sherlock.

The 13th Clue by Ann Jonas (Greenwillow Books). Pictorial clues lead to a big surprise.

Party Favor

Fill plain brown lunch bags with candy, chocolate coins, perhaps a decoder ring, a plastic mini-maze, a puzzle or riddle book, a magnifying glass, and play money. Write $$$ on the bag, and cinch the top with twine.

"IT WORKED FOR ME"

"I avoid any petty jealousy or special request by making sure everybody's slice of cake and everybody's goody bag is exactly the same. This applies to things like cupcakes as well—I resist the temptation to decorate each differently, and so make them all alike."

Arty Party

Color your birthday child happy with a celebration of creativity. Budding Picassos aged 6 and above will have the art-smarts and freedom of expression to make this event a wonder to behold. In the invitation, or at the time of the RSVPs, ask guests to bring a smock or paint shirt. Let the kids draw on their imaginations and you'll send them home with a masterpiece or two.

Invitation
Fashion a painter's palette cut from manila folders. Glue on blobs of construction paper "paint" in assorted colors and add the necessary information.

Decorations
- Set up some "blank canvases" for kids to adorn: Put an old white sheet or heavy white paper tablecloth on the table, and spread a roll of paper on the ground or along a fence or an interior wall. The kids can decorate these during the party, or you and your child can decorate the tablecloth ahead of time (see Party Starters, following page).
- Spread dropcloths on the floor or ground. The more paint-spattered, the better.
- Cluster art supplies: paint bottles in baskets, brushes or markers in tin cans.
- Set out postcards or posters of work by well-known artists, which can be purchased from cata-

logs and museum gift shops. Works by Alexander Calder, Henri Matisse, Keith Haring, and Jackson Pollack can all serve as inspiration.

Party Starters

Asphalt Art
Have the kids use sidewalk chalk to draw on the driveway or patio.

Bring Art to the Table
Ask each child to decorate a designated portion of the tablecloth with handprints, foam stamps, potato prints, oodles of doodles from paint pens. (Spin in the dryer for 10 minutes to heat-set the paint, and you'll have artwork-in-progress for several birthdays to come.)

Giant Mural
Unfurl a big roll of paper along a wall or the floor. Let everyone work on it. Suggest that some kids make funny poses, and others trace around them.

Activities

Wacky Self-Portraits
Demonstrate the technique before you launch this activity. Hang clear acetate sheets on a big mirror with tape. As each kid peers at herself, she marks her features with a permanent marker. Have the kids untape their drawings and fill in every area with a color that's not at all

true to life, using neon acrylic paints and a paintbrush. Let these portraits dry, at least a bit, then glue them to the cover of a folder they'll take home.

Architectural Sculptures

Beforehand: Provide a sheet of plywood, measuring about ¼" × 12" × 15", for each child. Also provide wood glue and a big bin of assorted wood shapes: blocks, cubes, domes, finials, wheels, pegs, craft sticks, and other pieces of pine or balsa.

At the party: Let the kids arrange the wood shapes on the plywood. When they're satisfied with the total effect, have them use wood glue to secure each component. If time allows, they may paint the results with washable acrylics.

For another variation of this activity, have the artists collaborate on a larger sculpture using cardboard containers such as empty food cartons, paper towel and toilet paper tubes, and egg crates. Kids can use masking tape, craft glue, or, if supervised, low-temperature glue guns to join the pieces.

PARENTS ALERT

Check all wood pieces to be sure they're smooth before passing them out. Sand edges of plywood, or coat them with white glue.

Modernist Mobile

Put out craft foam in assorted colors, colored yarn or string, clothes hangers, chalk, several pairs of child-safe scissors, and a hole punch. Let kids cut shapes to pierce and dangle on various lengths of string from a hanger. A big circle, with a spiral cut into it, will contribute great movement to the piece; squares may be slit halfway and fitted into each other for another 3-D element.

PARENTS ALERT

Cover the hoop end of wire coat hangers with masking tape to prevent accidental scrapes. Plastic hangers are a safer choice.

Food

Paint-Palette Cake

Depending upon the number of guests, bake a sheet cake or a single-layer round cake. When it is cool, use a serrated knife to trim the sides, creating a paint-palette shape; also cut out a thumb hole. Transfer the cake to a serving platter. Ice with pale yellow icing and, to make pools of paint, add dots or squiggles of icing tinted with food coloring, flattened gumdrops, or colorful candy wafers. Place the appropriate number of candles on the cake.

Abstract-Art Ice Cream

Fill squeeze bottles with various ice cream sauces such as raspberry, caramel, chocolate sauce, and fruit jelly thinned with water and set them out. Cut each child a slice from a brick of vanilla ice cream. Encourage the kids to dribble and draw over their own serving, using any or all sauces. Efforts may be painterly or totally wild!

Story Time

Harold and the Purple Crayon by Crocket Johnson (Scholastic). As Harold shows, an artist can be master of his fate.

The Art Lesson by Tomie de Paola (Paper Star). The author/illustrator looks back on his first crack at art class.

Party Favor

Tuck a few art supplies into each self-portrait folder: Consider a pad of paper and a few colored pencils, a jigsaw puzzle you've made by cutting apart a large postcard, or a few pieces of origami paper with a photocopy of an instruction sheet.

"IT WORKED FOR ME"

"My child really enjoys crafts projects, so I always have a run-through of any we plan for the party. This way I'm sure the kids can handle the activity, and I know my daughter will have the confidence to help."

ANTICIPATION AND LETDOWN

Right before and after a party is a very stressful time for the birthday child—which often means

ANTICIPATION AND LETDOWN

that it's no picnic for the parent! The anticipation, especially for a younger child who has an unrealistic sense of time, is compounded by anxiety (will anyone show up?) and last-minute frenzy. Afterwards, it's only natural that the child feels wound up or let down—or both. Handling these periods is just as important as running a good party.

Put the Birthday Child in a Party Mood

- Make your birthday boy or girl feel special as early in the day as possible. Waking up to a special greeting, gift, or breakfast will color her mood for the rest of the day.

- Try not to leave party preparations to the last minute.

- Find ways your child can help set up for the party. For instance, let her assemble the goody bags or make and put out place cards.

- Before the party, have your child pick out certain toys that he doesn't mind sharing, which can stay out. More importantly, suggest he safely store those possessions he doesn't want others to touch.

- Direct your child's attention to the feelings of the other children who will be attending. That will get his mind off his worries. Your child is a host as much as you are. Rehearse some lines your child can say to make guests feel welcome and good about the gifts they brought. That way, your child will feel comfortable with gift-receiving (and gift-opening, if you choose to do this).

- If you're having an afternoon party that doesn't include a meal, go out for lunch! Relax at a fast-food restaurant where you won't have to worry about food preparation and extra cleanup.

"IT WORKED FOR ME"

"I practice gift-opening time with my child by handing him a toy and having him look me right in the eye and say thank you. I also coach him on nice things he could say if he receives something he already has, or something that he really doesn't want."

Prevent Those Post-Party Blues
- Discourage anyone from staying past the allotted time of the party. Your birthday child will probably need time alone, maybe vegging out in front of a video. The exception to this is if one of the guests is a special, simpático buddy with a laid-back disposition. After a big group hullabaloo, your child might enjoy some quiet one-on-one with one special friend—or with a family member.

- A compliment often disarms a child and keeps her from pouting. Reinforce what a wonderful hostess she was, or how proud you were that she was so nice to her friends.

- If presents were not opened during the party, quickly gratify your child's need to see what was brought. Jot down who brought what as you ooh and aah over the bounty.

- Reassure your child that a duplicate gift can be exchanged, or given to someone else at another party.

- Put off cleaning everything up. Allow your child to play with one or two of the gifts; join her if she seems receptive.

- Try not to schedule anything after the party, including a dinner at grandma's house. Lessen the other social obligations of the day so that your child can decompress.

"IT WORKED FOR ME"

"Although my daughter is always anxious to tear into any craft kits she receives, I encourage her to put this off until I can help her. At a later date we'll both have more time (and patience) to enjoy these projects. Instead, I direct her attention to less involved gifts. We also have fun reviewing the party together, remembering the funny moments and the activities that were the biggest hits."

Nature Lovers Unlimited

Invite little explorers to a walk in your local wilderness. A park with a nature center is the perfect site to hold this party for kids 6 or older, but a neighborhood patch of woods will suffice. Recruit a few parent chaperones to keep an eye on wanderers, and suggest proper clothing and footwear. This party is dependent on Mother Nature's cooperation, so be sure to supply a rain or snow date.

Invitation

Send suncatchers! Ask your child to help gather pretty leaves small enough to fit in an envelope. To flatten, sandwich each leaf between sheets of wax paper, and then place it between paper towels. Press, using a dry iron, and remove the paper. Seal one to two leaves between two envelope-size pieces of clear self-adhesive vinyl. Use a hole punch to make a hole, and add a length of string for hanging. Prepare paper invitations with the words: "We wouldn't LEAF you out! Come to Jessie's birthday party for nature lovers!" Add the party particulars.

Decorations

- Purchase minimal, natural, recycled paper tableware.
- Cover the table with a big sheet of brown paper; if the food will be served outdoors, use large rocks as paperweights. Cut huge leaves from green crêpe

paper for place mats; tape them down if necessary.
Use real leaves as decorative coasters under the
cups.

- Start a giant, natural poster to which everyone can
contribute: Use sidewalk chalk on a stone or as-
phalt surface, and let kids punctuate and embellish
the design with stones, acorns, twigs, leaves, and
other natural objects. Or, simply use sticks to write
messages in the dirt or sand. Be sure to get permis-
sion from the nature center first.

Party Starters

Arrange to meet at the site where you will hike. While
you are waiting for the late arrivals, give each child a
brown lunch bag "collector's sack" and let him write his
name on it. Also supply each child with a small four-
pack of crayons and a clear plastic box with a magnifying glass in the lid. Suggest that they immediately use
the crayons and decorate the bag by making a bark rubbing or by tracing leaves. Talk about the different tex-
tures and shapes that the kids discover. The kids should
put the crayons and boxes inside their bags.

Activities

1-2-3 Hike!

Beforehand: Choose a trail and preview it. A short
loop is the best, anywhere from ¼ mile for
younger children up to 1 mile for the older ones.
If possible, demarcate the trail by tying ribbon
around trees, but be sure to remove the ribbons
afterwards. Acquire several pairs of binoculars.

Educate yourself about the flora and fauna, or secure the services of a park guide.

At the party: Pair up buddies and request that everyone stay with the group, then head off into the woods. Point out frogs, insects, small wildlife, and birds. Give everyone a chance to look through binoculars. Let the kids place an ant, a beetle, or a little leaf in their boxes to study through the magnifier; afterwards, ask that they return the living creatures close to where they found them. After all, bugs want to stay near their families—or at least their sources of food. The kids will point out many wonderful things. Be flexible, allow the kids to determine the pace as much as possible, and let nature do the entertaining.

Scavenger Hunt

If you wish, the scavenger hunt can be incorporated into the hike. If the children are older and there are enough adults to keep an eye on them, you can hold it separately.

Beforehand: Choose several items for the children to search out, selecting from or adapting the following list as appropriate for your hiking spot. (Check with the park administration for any rules about scavenging.) Prepare a poster with the items glued on, and draw the same objects on file cards to pass out. You might challenge the kids to find or make:

- Tracings of three different types of leaves
- A bark rubbing
- A drawing or name of an animal sighted

- A pine cone
- An acorn
- Several thin twigs
- A pebble or small rock
- A feather
- A drawing of animal tracks discovered

At the party: Ask kids to find these items and place them in their bags. Explain that they must obey the rules of the park or preserve and not pick flowers or leaves off plants: Every item they put in their sacks must already be on the ground.

Signs of Nature

When you return to base (or go back to your home if you plan to serve refreshments there), let the children work on some wonderfully rustic markers. They will look great hanging on a porch, a tree outside the house, or on the door or wall of a kid's room.

You need:
- Drill and ⅜" bit
- Pine or balsa wood, 6" × 8" × ⅛" piece for each
- Sandpaper
- Cord or twine, 24" length for each
- Natural items such as mini pine cones, acorn caps, chips of bark, gravel, twigs
- Pencils
- Craft glue

Beforehand: Drill two holes centered along one long edge on each board. Sand the boards to prevent splinters. Put natural items into small baskets or boxes, in case the kids don't collect enough.

At the party: Have the kids thread cord into the holes and knot the ends to form a hanging loop. Help them to lightly pencil their names or their house numbers on the board in big, block characters. Let kids arrange natural items over the marked characters, and then apply glue to the back of each item and replace it. Allow the signs to dry until the kids depart.

Food

In the event that you'll be serving refreshments at a park or woodsy site, you'll need a menu of items that are portable, need no refrigeration, and are easy to handle— preferably finger food. But first, after all that contact with lots of wonderfully dirty items, kids will need an opportunity to clean their hands. If sinks and soap are not convenient, offer packaged wipes or dabs of sanitizing hand lotion so they can "wash up" without water.

Trail Mix

Blend breakfast cereal, candy morsels, cut-up dates, figs, banana chips, and pretzel nuggets.

Birthday Bars

Set squares of these healthful, delicious bars so they nestle around a big column candle. However, if Smokey the Bear has an objection, you can all sing "Happy Birthday" with a lighted flashlight!

In a large bowl, mix together 3 cups uncooked oatmeal,

1½ cups flour, 1 cup brown sugar, 1 cup melted margarine, ¾ teaspoon salt, and ½ teaspoon baking soda. Set aside 1 cup of this mixture, and press the remainder into a greased 9" × 13" baking pan. Spread all the fruit preserves from a 10- or 12-ounce jar over the top, leaving a ½" margin around the edges empty. Sprinkle on the reserved crumbs and bake at 350°F for 25 to 30 minutes. Cool, then cut into bars.

Story Time

The Giving Tree by Shel Silverstein (Harper-Collins). An apple tree has much to offer a little boy throughout his life.

Red Leaf, Yellow Leaf by Louise Ehlert (Harcourt Brace). Follow a maple tree from seed to sapling.

Party Favor

Add a few sweets or trinkets to the kids' nature bags—if your nature center sells bits of polished rock or botanical postcards, they'd be great. Add the decorated signs.

Hooray for Hollywood!

Here's the script for a party where every child is a star. The focus of this party is a home movie the kids create and then watch at a private screening party. Most kids 7 and over are sophisticated enough to appreciate this theme, and self-assured enough to provide some dramatic mugging in front of a camera. You'll need adult help, so pull friends into the act.

Invitation

With white construction paper and a gold paint pen, you can make "fancy" Hollywood invitations for the guests. Prepare invitations with the words: "You're Invited to a Movie Premiere—Starring You!" Then add the party particulars.

Decorations

- Cut big letters from white foam board that spell HOLLYWOOD, like the giant sign on the Hollywood hills in Los Angeles. Tape a stake behind each letter. If the party is outdoors, pound these stakes into the ground. If the party is indoors, tape the stakes so that the letters extend from behind the sofa.
- Ask for old posters at your local video store and hang them.
- Hang or set out every item you've got (or can borrow) with a movie actor or movie cartoon charac-

ter: T-shirts, towels, stuffed animals, lunch boxes, baseball caps, magazines.

- Use paper goods from the party store that display movie characters.
- Buy or cut out big, shiny, glittery paper star shapes and spread them everywhere.
- Make a collage with pages torn from a movie magazine and a snapshot of the birthday child, showing her in the company of her favorite movie stars.
- Make EXIT, ON AIR, QUIET ON THE SET signs to put over the doors and on walls, just like at a real movie or TV studio.

Party Starters

Sidewalk Stars

Along the Walk of Fame on Hollywood Boulevard in Hollywood, celebrities are given a square of cement to sign and imprint with a hand. At this party, everyone is a movie star!

You need:
- Cutting boards
- Cellophane wrap
- White air-drying clay
- 1 cup of sand in a natural color
- Small wood star
- Toothpicks

Beforehand: Cover a couple of cutting boards with cellophane or plastic wrap. Roll clay out on each board to a ¼" thickness, and sprinkle sand on top to create the look of cement. Use a paring knife and ruler to cut a grid of 7" squares; don't separate the squares. Center the star on each square and press (or tap with a small hammer) to make a slight impression. Cover the slabs with cellophane so that they will remain workable until all the guests arrive.

At the party: Have each child push one or both hands into the clay on a square slab. Let her sign her name using a toothpick. Let the squares dry during the party. When it's time for the kids to go home, separate the squares with a wide spatula, set each on a paper dinner plate, and hand them out.

Movie Makers

If you don't own a camcorder, borrow or rent one. Press an older sibling or teenage helper into service as your cameraperson. As the parent of the birthday child, you could be the director, but it's best if you can delegate this important job, leaving yourself available to host the party and produce the entire show. Seek out an adult with a flair for drama and an openness to children's imaginative input.

Beforehand: Work with your child to choose a short story or fairy tale that the group will produce. Look for a story with the same number of characters as the guests you expect, so that everyone can have at least a small part. Prepare some simple costumes and props, making use of old clothes, hats, Halloween masks and costumes. You might also write signboards for the title, scenes, and any key dialogue. Make a plan of action with the director (so that she can keep the action moving) and cameraperson (so that he knows to focus on the signboards at opportune moments).

Here are a few ideas:
- The Three Billy Goats Gruff
- Cinderella and the Glass Slipper
- Hansel and Gretel
- Rip Van Winkle
- The Three Wolves and the Big Bad Pig (Ha!)

Quickie Rehearsal

If someone is not in an early scene, have that child illustrate the signboards or make borders to decorate them. Go over the story and let the kids ad-lib their way through it once or twice.

Lights! Camera! Action!

Film the story. The ideal camcorder for this party would allow for rewinding and taping over the less successful moments. The director should announce each scene "a wrap" after a few minutes so that the story reaches its end before the performers run out of steam. Remember to insert the signboards into the project.

The Private Screening

Invite everyone to gather in front of the TV to watch their movie. It may be an unedited series of "dailies," but it's sure to delight the entire cast. OK, it may be awful—try showing it in reverse. Depending on time and patience level, you may wish to follow this up with a selection from the video rental store and skip story time for this party.

The Awards Ceremony

Beforehand: Make statuette awards: Purchase papier-mâché bowling pins or angel figures and spray-paint them gold. Or, cut a 10"-high silhouette figure from gold poster board and support it with a poster board base that slits perpendicularly in place. In either case, use a black marker to add some simple facial features, crossed arms, and a straight line to divide the legs.

At the party: Give each child a figurine to honor individual work on the production. Pronounce him "Best Actor," "Funniest Performer," "Scariest Villain," and so on. Allow each child up to one minute to give an acceptance speech. Take pictures with a flash camera.

Food

Screening Room Snacks

- Popcorn in paper cups
- Soda in paper cups with lids and straws

- Single-serving packets of the kinds of snacks movie theaters carry—chocolate-covered raisins, chocolates covered with nonpareils, chocolate-covered mints, soft pretzel bites

Ceremonious Fare

Glass of bubbly: Lemon-lime soda or ginger ale in plastic champagne glasses.

Story Time

Bantam of the Opera by Mary Jane Auch (Holiday House). In this story, Luigi, a lowly farm rooster, dreams of life as an opera star. He gets his big break when a traveling opera company comes to town. The tenor and the tenor's understudy have suddenly come down with chicken pox, leading the way to Luigi's successful debut.

Albert Goes to Hollywood by Henry Schwartz (Orchard). Albert the dinosaur is happy serving the PTA as an educational consultant, but he's eating them out of house and home and he's got to go. His friend Liz has an idea: Take him to Hollywood where he can be discovered and where, as a star of the big screen, he can be self supporting.

Party Favor

Kids will be very proud to take home their awards and their sidewalk squares.

COUNTDOWN TO THE BIG DAY

Four Weeks Before
- Set the date.

- Book any entertainment. (You may have to book popular acts months in advance, so check before mentioning it to your child.)

- Make or buy invitations. Fill out (including RSVP date) and mail or deliver. A month gives parents time to check schedules.

Three Weeks Before
- Read through your party plan and make a shopping list of all supplies and groceries.

- Shop for tabletop paper goods.

- Order any special supplies.

Two Weeks Before
- Start making or buying decorations. Figure out how you'll rig any that need hanging or other support.

- Stock up on whatever supplies will be needed for craft projects.

- Shop for goody bags and prizes.

COUNTDOWN TO THE BIG DAY

One Week Before
- Enlist the help of other parents or older siblings to chaperone the party.

- Call any parent who hasn't responded.

- Check your cameras for film and flash. Do a test run with your camcorder.

The Day Before
- Purchase food. Bake or buy cake. Prepare any other food that can be safely made ahead.

- Child-proof the party area.

- Run through each activity. Organize props.

Party Day
- Make the food.

- Set up indoor decorations, blow up balloons, and step back to observe.

- Set up outdoor activities and decorations.

- Set up the party starters (the first arrival activities) or any necessary craft stations.

- Make a pot of coffee for any adults who linger.

- Chill extra juice, soda, and milk.

Alakazam!

Really! Nothing up your sleeve but a good time for all. Children 7 or older make a great audience, and they'll be thrilled with and capable of learning and practicing these amazing magic tricks. We bet their friends and families will be thrilled, too, when the guests take their new skills home!

Invitation

Send out a top hat with a rabbit that pops out! Here's how: On white paper, draw a simple top hat shape and write on it "Can you make the rabbit appear? Now, can you make yourself appear for Julian's 8th birthday party?" and add all the party particulars. Also draw a rabbit that will fit in the crown of the hat. Photocopy this as needed and cut out. From black paper, cut out a second hat for each invitation and in it cut a slit where the brim meets the crown. Gluing around the edges only, glue a black hat to the wrong side of each white one. Insert a rabbit in each hat.

Decorations

- Cut stars and lightning bolts from foil poster board and tape them to the walls.
- Tie all your colorful scarves (or 18" squares of lining fabric) together at diagonal corners to form a long garland. Hang them in swags across ceiling

hooks or light fixtures, with one end disappearing into a plastic top hat (from the party store) in the center of a table.
- On the dining table, cluster more plastic top hats. Place a bunch of artificial flowers in one, snack foods in the others.

Party Starters

Magic Wands
You need:
- ¾" diameter wood dowels, cut into 12" lengths
- Sandpaper
- Black acrylic paint
- Paintbrushes
- Quick-setting craft glue
- Glitter in one or more colors, poured into paper cups

Beforehand: Sand the dowels, smoothing the cut ends thoroughly. Cover the worktable with newspaper. Set out the paintbrushes, paint, glue, and glitter. Round up some old shirts or aprons so that clothing stays clean. Make a wand for yourself to use at the party.

At the party: Have each kid paint a dowel with two coats of black paint and then let it dry for a few minutes. Next, have each kid apply glue to one end of his dowel and dip this end into a cup of glitter. Suggest that the kids leave a bit of space, then paint a band of glue around the wand and sprinkle the same or a different glitter over this band. If they wish, the kids may continue to add glittery bands or other patterns. Set the wands aside to dry.

PARENTS ALERT

If there will be toddlers at the party, cut some "magic wands" from heavy paper and give the toddlers crayons to use for decorating; you can add glitter when they are finished.

Activities

Demonstrate each of these tricks once or twice. Let the kids try to guess the secrets before you teach them how each is done. Let them know: "Practice makes perfect!" (This applies to you, too.)

The Rising Cube

Place a small strip of paper napkin over an ice cube. Say: "I can pull the ice cube up with this strip!" Take the ends of the strip and lift it; of course, the ice cube won't come with it. Say: "Oh dear, I need a little magic. First, the magic fairy dust!" Sprinkle the magic dust over the ice cube. Smooth the strip over the ice cube. Wave the magic wand over the ice cube three times, and utter a magic chant of some sort. This time, the ice cube will elevate along with the strip.

The Secret: The magic fairy dust is salt, which, given a little time, makes the ice melt and refreeze, sticking it to the paper.

The Disappearing Drink

On a table, place two brown lunch bags, a small pitcher of water, and a rimless, opaque disposable cup. Place the cup in the bag on your left. Fill the cup with water from the pitcher, letting everyone see the flow of water. Say, "I will now make the cup of water fly into the paper bag on my right." Laughter ensues as you carefully lift the cup out of one bag and lower it into the other. "Now," you announce, "I will make the water disappear!" Wave the magic wand over the right bag, blabber a few magic words, and carefully pick up the bag, as if to avoid spilling the water. Look inside, and exclaim, "It's gone!" To prove your statement, crush the bag—there will be no seepage—and toss it away. Ask your audience, "Where do you think it has gone?" Point to the other sack: "Here it is!" Remove the cup with water. Prove that there's been no spillage by pouring the water back into the pitcher.

The Secret: There was an identical but bottomless cup inside the cup that was shown. What was lifted out of the first bag was merely the empty, bottomless cup. The filled outer cup remained in the first bag.

The Sticky Spoon

Ask each kid to hold a plastic spoon on his nose. Not many noses can handle this challenge! But you hold a spoon up to your face and say, "Hocus-pocus, ha-ha-ha!" and then press the concave side of the spoon on your nose—and it stays!

The Secret: The breathy, exhaled incantation provides a mist that helps the spoon stick in place.

The Mind Reader

The mind reader goes out of the room, and while she is gone, the guests select some object in the room. The mind reader is invited back, and must guess what item was chosen by peering into the minds of the kids. Meanwhile, the birthday child points to various objects and asks, "Is it this one? Is it this? Is it this thing over here?" to which the mind reader replies, "No" each time. The birthday child then points to the chosen item and asks, "Is it that?" The mind reader then says "Yes" and is, in fact, correct.

The Secret: The mind reader and the birthday child are in cahoots. Whenever the birthday child says, "Is it this?" the answer is no, but when the word "that" is used, the mind reader has the necessary hint.

A Penny Out of Thin Air

This trick is from the late, great entertainer, Shari Lewis: Start by boasting, "I'm such a good magician, I can find money anywhere, even on my elbow!" Show your empty hands. With your left hand, rub your right elbow. Unfortunately, this does not prove successful, so you say, "Whoops, wrong elbow." Then you rub your left elbow and, lo and behold, a coin comes out!

The Secret: Beforehand, you've hidden a coin in the crook of your left arm, and you've kept both arms bent just enough to keep the coin in place. When you say, "Whoops, wrong elbow," you grab the hidden coin with the fingers of your right hand, and make it appear as if you pulled it out of your elbow.

The Wizard's Wand

One child plays the wizard, and is outfitted in a cone-shaped party hat, covered with star stickers. The wizard uses the wand she made earlier. Everyone else prances around making all sorts of crazy movements. As soon as the wizard gently touches someone's shoulder with the wand, that person must freeze in whatever position he or she happens to be in. This continues until the wizard has frozen all but one person. That one becomes the magician, who receives a plastic top hat and who uses his wand to unfreeze kids. If he works in the same order as the wizard, the kids will all have a chance to see and laugh at everyone else's funny positions. The last person unfrozen becomes the new wizard.

Food

Apple-cadabra

Find two apples in different colors (such as a red delicious and a Granny Smith) that are roughly the same size and shape. Use an apple corer to core each one and reserve these cores. Slice each piece of fruit horizontally into several slices, and brush lemon juice on the slices, to prevent them from turning brown. Stack the slices together over the core, alternating apple types so you have stripes of different color peel.

Magic Mix

Combine thin pretzel wands, raisins, and breakfast cereal with marshmallow charm shapes.

PARENTS ALERT

If there will be toddlers at the party, omit the raisins from the mix.

Pick a Card, Any Card Ice Cream Sandwiches

For the cookie part, mix up a butter cookie or short-bread dough. Roll it out, and cut it into 3" × 4" rectangles. Transfer these rectangles to a cookie sheet. Round the corners of each rectangle, so that each has the shape of a playing card. Bake according to your recipe, and let cool. With decorator icing, turn half the cookies into aces: Use black icing for spades and clubs, red for hearts and diamonds. Screw on a writing tip to squeeze out an A in the upper left corner, then turn the cookie 180 degrees and make an A diagonally opposite the first. Outline a big spade, club, heart, or diamond in the middle; you could use a star tip to fill in the shape. Let the icing set for about an hour until hard. To assemble the sandwiches, lay out the undecorated cookies. Slice 3" × 4" pieces from a brick of ice cream, ½" to ¾" thick, and layer on these cookies. Top with a decorated cookie. Place in one layer on a cookie sheet in the freezer; remove a few minutes before serving.

Story Time

Sylvester and the Magic Pebble by William Steig (Simon & Schuster). Wishes come true to ill effect for a little donkey.

Strega Nona's Magic Lessons by Tomie de Paola (Harcourt Brace). An endearing little witch casts spells.

Jack and the Beanstalk. Any edition of this classic tale. Magic beans lead to a big adventure in the sky.

Party Favor

From a magic, variety, or party store, select little magic-trick gadgets—the same for everyone: metal rings that don't seem to separate, or a ball that disappears into a little cup; you'll find these packaged with directions for use. Place the tricks in small silver or gold gift bags. You can help kids decipher the directions and practice until it's time to disappear—that is, when their parents show up and take them (and their magic wands) home!

"IT WORKED FOR ME"

"At the end of a party, enthusiastic guests overwhelmed my child by thrusting their gifts on him at the same time. So this year I turned opening presents into a game: "Spin the Bottle"—without kissing. My child does the first spin, and whomever the bottle points to gets up, finds the gift he brought, and gives it to my child to open. That guest spins the bottle next."

Backyard Carnival

Hurry, hurry, hurry! Step right up! Everyone's a winner at this down-home country fair! For a joyous party that caters to kids of all ages, set up a fairway with lots of booths and games. Smaller children (or smaller numbers of children) can work their way down the fairway together. Otherwise, some help from teens or adults will allow for lots of simultaneous activity. Award the kids tickets for every success—even for good behavior!

Invitation

Draw or create a collage of a clown head on light-weight card stock; cut it out and cut a slit in its mouth. Unfurl a party blower and write all the information along it; insert the end into the mouth of the clown. Deliver the invitations by hand or mail them in padded envelopes.

Decorations

- A ticket booth at the entrance, where every guest receives five (or whatever age the birthday child may be) free tickets to start collecting toward prizes. For an outdoor party, make the booth banner from cutout foam board and sturdy dowels; indoors hang a felt banner in a doorway.
- Pennants, tent stripes—use crêpe paper—and lots of Mylar balloons!
- Circus barker hats (flat-topped, flat-brimmed plas-

tic or foam "boaters," as they are often called) for anyone who wants to wear one.

Party Starters

As guests arrive, let them immediately choose from face painting, press-on tattoos, or filling up small bags of pretzel sticks from a big bowl.

Activities

Ring Toss

Beforehand: For rings, cut 1½"-wide strips along the length of a 22" × 28" sheet of brightly colored poster board. Overlap the ends and staple; tape over the staples for safe handling. For goals, push dowels into the ground, or set out plastic soda bottles filled with water or sand. Ask the birthday child to help you figure out how far from the goal the children should stand when they toss the paper rings, and mark this spot. Older kids may toss rubber gaskets (used in canning) over the dowels.

To play: Give each child several rings to toss over the dowels. Let each child have a turn before allowing repeats.

PARENTS ALERT

Don't let the kids run unattended near the dowel goals.

Down the Clown

Beforehand: Put about 2" of water in each of three
to five empty plastic soda bottles. Screw on the
caps and push a plastic foam ball "head" onto the
top of each. Glue on felt, pom-poms, and curling
ribbon for facial features and wigs; add stickers
and ribbons for a suit, and use cone-shaped water
cooler cups for hats.

To play: Line the clowns up across a bench or
table and, one at a time, let the kids take aim
with a Wiffle ball.

Feed the Clown

Beforehand: On a 30" × 40" piece of foam board,
paint a silly clown head with a large, open smile.
Using a craft knife, cut out the smile. Tape another piece of foam board to the back for an
easel stand, or lean the board against a sturdy
chair or a sawhorse. (If setting up outdoors, secure the board by wedging the bottom with plastic soda bottles filled with sand.) You can sew
some simple bean bags for kids to throw, ask the
guests to bring their bean-bag toys from home,
or provide mini flying disks.

To play: Age determines how far back a child stands
to aim and throw toward the clown's mouth. Let
each child have a turn before allowing repeats.

Have a Ball

Prop up three laundry baskets at an angle—support each
on a stack of magazines or a phone book. Have each
child stand in front of a basket and try to toss a ball into

it. The younger the child, the larger the ball, but in any case, balls will tend to bounce out of the baskets, adding to the challenge of getting one in.

Food

Veggie Ring Toss

Insert a large carrot or celery stick into the center of a sheet of plastic foam. Decorate the edges of the foam with ribbon. Slice rings of red, yellow, and green peppers; stack them on the carrot or celery stick and let the kids serve themselves.

Roller-Coaster Franks

Purchase a tube of refrigerated soft breadsticks and a package of hot dogs. Preheat the oven to 400°F; shape each breadstick in an S-curve and place it on a baking sheet. Bake, following package directions, cool, and slice lengthwise in half, using a serrated knife. Using a paring knife, make ½"-deep slits across each hot dog at ½" intervals; when you've cut along half the length, rotate the hot dog and slash from the opposite side. Simmer in boiling water for 5 minutes, or until curvy. Serve on the curvy breadsticks with choice of condiments.

Fairway Fruit Salad

Drain a 16-ounce can of pineapple chunks, reserving the juice. Combine the chunks with mandarin orange sections and apple slices; add some of the reserved pineapple juice to prevent the apples from discoloring, and stir to combine. Chill. Just before serving, add ½ cup of colored, mini marshmallows.

Juggler Cake

Make one round cake and enough cupcakes for each child to have one. Frost and decorate the cake as a clown face, using decorator icing, cookies, and candies for funny features; use string licorice for hair and/or an ice cream cone at a jaunty angle for a hat. Use food coloring to tint the cupcake frosting a bright color (the same color for everyone will avoid conflicts). Arrange the cake on a big tray, placing a bright fabric bow tie below the chin, a glove to either side, and an arch of cupcakes at the top.

Story Time

Henrietta Goes to the Fair by Syd Hoff (Garrand Publishing Company). The farmer expects his pig to win a prize at the fair, and Henrietta the hen goes along.

The Berenstain Bears Ride the Thunderbolt by Stan and Jan Berenstain (Random House). The bear family rides a roller coaster.

Party Favor

Let the kids turn in their tickets for their choices of penny candy, little plastic trinkets, little balls, pinwheels, funny erasers, mini noisemakers, and other treasures. Booty may be carried home in the barker hats or in paper bags with stripes reminiscent of a carnival tent.

Pizzeria

Kids create their own pies to double the fun of this pizza party. Almost all kids like helping in the kitchen and eating pizza—particularly when they pick their own toppings. Protect the front of each "chef's" clothing with an improvised apron made from paper towels secured with masking tape. That way, you'll be sending the guests home clean and happy.

Invitation

Create a paper slice of pizza with all the information written on top. Make photocopies of the original and then let your child color with crayons or colored pencils and, if she's 5 or older, cut out the wedge shape.

Decorations

- Make a restaurant sign that says "Martha's Pizza Parlor."
- Hang red, white, and green streamers from the sign.
- Make Italian flags from red, white, and green tissue paper strips, and hang them on string stretched across the party area.
- Cover tables with red-and-white checked tablecloths.

Party Starters

Play-Clay Pizzas

For a small group of young children, make play clay (recipe on page 131) and let the kids practice kneading and squeezing dough. Or, buy or borrow a "Play-Doh Pizza Parlor" by Kenner, featuring molds for making various ingredients.

Chef Hats

You need:

- 4" × 17" strips of white construction paper, for hat bands
- Sheets of white tissue paper
- Markers or crayons
- Food stickers or food magazines and glue sticks
- Clear tape

1. Let the kids write their names on the construction-paper hat bands and decorate them with stickers or pictures of foods cut from magazines. Test-fit each child's band, overlap the ends, and tape them.
2. To make each hat crown, fold a sheet of tissue paper in half crosswise. Tape across the side edges that are next to the fold, forming a little bag.
3. Gently turn the bag inside out. Tape the open edges inside a hat band, making small pleats in the tissue paper as you go around.

Food

Personal Pies

Beforehand: Cut aluminum foil into 6" squares. Divide prepared pizza dough (from the frozen or refrigerator case at the supermarket) into balls. You could also use English muffins, pocket bread, foccaccia, or any flat bread for crust.

At the party: Give each child a foil square, pizza dough or some flat bread, a small paper cup filled with tomato sauce, and a small plastic spoon. Put out bowls of shredded cheese, slices of pepperoni, diced green pepper, and even some unusual toppings ... like pineapple chunks or raisins. Ask the kids to flatten the circle of dough on their foil square, then add toppings. Caution them, "This is going to be yours to eat, so choose only the toppings that you like!" After lifting the foil onto cookie sheets, use a toothpick or permanent marker to write each child's name on the appropriate piece of foil. Bake at 350°F for 6 to 10 minutes and serve!

PARENTS ALERT

Make sure all toppings are cut and diced to prevent choking.

Dessert Pizzas

- Form a roll of refrigerator cookie dough into a ball, then flatten it into a giant cookie on a baking sheet. Bake. Put out decorator icing, gumdrops, small candy-coated chocolates, and other candies and let the kids decorate.

- Bake a flat, ready-made pie crust. Spread it with cream cheese, softened and thinned with milk, and lay sliced fruit on top. Make a glaze by heating ½ cup of apricot preserves, and spread it thinly over the fruit.
- For either dessert pizza, use a squatty number candle or place tea lights all around.

Activities

Pizza Delivery

Divide kids into two or more small teams. Give each team a Frisbee or large paper plate decorated to resemble a pizza. Each team member must balance this item on his head and move quickly to a cone or marker and then pass the "pizza" to the next person on the team. Continue until all have had a turn.

Slice Magnets

Beforehand: Cut out small wedges for "pizza crusts" from plastic foam trays. Cut "sauce" triangles from red construction paper. Using colored craft foam, cut brown "pepperoni rounds," tan "mushroom slices," and green "pepper strips." Also cut white yarn into 2" strands of "cheese." Set out all these items at the work area.

At the party: Have the kids choose their ingredients, then assemble their pizza slices with glue. Glue a magnet strip to the back of each slice, and everyone will have a self-made refrigerator magnet as a prize!

Story Time

Cloudy with a Chance of Meatballs by Judith Barrett (Aladdin Paperbacks). A hilarious fable about food.

Little Nino's Pizzeria by Karen Barbour (Harcourt Brace). Takes you into the back to see how a small pizza restaurant operates.

Party Favor

Place some of the following in a bag and tie closed with curling ribbons of red, white, and green: scratch-and-sniff stickers for pizza, a wooden spoon with child's name on the handle, a little Italian flag pick, a twirly straw, a plastic bag of play clay (recipe on page 131).

"IT WORKED FOR ME"

"I use RSVP time as my opportunity to let parents know that my husband and I prefer that our child not have any toy guns or other weapons."

Happy Trails

Pitch a daytime campout in your own backyard. Even urbanites can simulate a mini camping trip (decorate your family room if you don't have a yard). If, however, you've got access to a park or some woods, a nature walk would be a wonderful activity. Point out frogs, insects, small wildlife, and birds, and give everyone a chance to look through binoculars. Kids of all ages will enjoy this frolic.

Invitation

Fold construction paper in half. Attach a real leaf with a blob of glue or rubber cement. Write "Campsite Celebration" underneath the leaf. Inside, write the particulars of the party. Note: Don't make these invitations too far in advance—you don't want the leaves to dry out before they arrive in the mailboxes of your guests.

Decorations

- Using sidewalk chalk, mark a path of animal tracks leading to the party area.
- Make a phony campfire from rocks, logs, and red and yellow cellophane wrap.
- Set up a tent. If you don't have access to the real thing, devise one by draping a blanket over a card table or clothesline.
- Make a "Don't Feed the Bears" sign and place some teddy bears nearby.

Party Starters

Nature Frames
You need:
- Wood tongue depressors, 4 for each
- Twine, 18" length for each
- Craft glue in squeeze bottles
- Assorted natural objects from your yard or craft store: pebbles, dried flowers or pods, tiny pine cones, moss, sunflower seeds

> **Beforehand:** For each child, overlap 4 tongue depressors to form a square frame with the ends extending about 1" (the frame opening should fit an instant photograph). Glue them together and let them dry completely.
>
> **At the party:** As the kids arrive, help each to tie a twine hanging loop to the top corners of a frame. Encourage the kids to arrange and glue the florals around the frames. Let the completed frames dry. If you have the opportunity to take instant photographs during the party, tape them behind the frames just before the guests depart.

Activities

Sleeping Bag Races
In this version of sack races, use old pillowcases to simulate sleeping bags. Have the kids step into them, hold the edges, and jump to a finish line.

Go Fish

Beforehand: Make the fish and the fishing rods as
  follows: Make a pattern for a simple 4" × 6" fish
  shape and use it to cut six fish from each of
  three different colors of craft foam. Also cut out
  several 1" × 2" hook shapes and punch a hole
  near one end of each. Glue a small, round magnet to each side of each fish, for an eye. Glue a
  magnet to each hook shape. For each fishing
  rod, tie one end of a 36" length of household
  string to a 22"-long stick or dowel; tie the other
  end of the string through the hole in a hook.
  When the glue has dried, drop the fish into a big
  plastic basin or tub.

At the party: Let the small fry try to catch fish
  with their rods. For older children, you might
  designate a different value for each color fish,
  perhaps 3 points for each bluefish, 2 points for
  each pink salmon, 1 point for each whitefish.
  Have them compete for the best catch of the
  day.

Also consider: tent tag (with the tent as base),
leapfrog, and classic circle games around the "campfire," such as hot potato.

Vittles

Trail Mix

Make your own concoction of such foods as crunchy
breakfast cereal, mini pretzels, chocolate chips, and
raisins and other dried fruits.

PARENTS ALERT

If children under 4 will be eating the trail mix, limit the contents to cereal, pretzels, and chocolate chips.

Campsite Cake

Combine the traditional flavors of s'mores in this visually pleasing cake. To begin, stake out the campsite by icing a sheet cake with marshmallow cream tinted with green food coloring; reserve a third of the tinted marshmallow cream for trees, and to use as needed for "glue." Make a tent: At one end of the cake, lean two graham crackers together in an inverted V; prop them up with a pretzel stick, trimmed to fit at each end. Use pressed fruit snack food to cover the sides and to make front flaps. Make a campfire: In front of the tent outline a circle with pebble candies or jelly bean "rocks." Break pieces of pretzel rods or sticks to fill the center area. Slice orange, yellow, and red gummy fruit slices, and add these "flames." For trees, tint ½ cup of marshmallow cream a brighter green. Gently fold in a cup of cornflakes or other crisp cereal. Spoon the sticky mixture over one end of pretzel stick "trunks," then insert the trunks into the cake. Children under 4 should be served portions decorated only with marshmallow cream.

Story Time

Amelia Bedelia Goes Camping by Peggy Parish (Camelot Books). As always, Amelia follows instructions too precisely, starting with pitching the tent.

When I Go Camping with Grandma by Marion Dane Bauer (Bridgewater Books). Hiking, canoeing, fishing, cooking out—what can't Granny do?

Party Favor

Mess Kit: For each, align the rims of two thin green plastic bowls. Punch holes in two opposite sides of the rims. Enclose a party favor or two as suggested below, and tie the bowls closed with silver curling ribbon. For party favors, consider a mini flashlight, a compass, a whistle, a clear plastic box with a magnifying glass in the lid, a frog toy (variously available as a squirt gun, a glow-in-the-dark figure, a leaping frog with an atomizer to squeeze, and a metal clicker), a rubber snake, and a porcupine (Koosh) ball.

Zoobilee!

Kids will chirp, squawk, and roar their approval for a zoo party. Everyone will have a lion's share of fun at these festivities. This is a grrrrreat theme for even the youngest toddlers who are just learning the names of animals and the sounds they make. For older kids, be prepared with plenty of "Did you know?" facts about exotic animals.

Invitation

Make a zoo scene using your child's picture plus a collage of animal cutouts. Write "We need YOU for our zoo party!" and add party particulars. Make photocopies to send out.

Decorations

- Put up a sign that reads, "This Way to the Zoo."
- Hang posters of various animals; tape black streamer "cage bars" over each.
- Put out helium balloons with animal faces drawn on with felt-tip markers; keep the strings short so small fry won't be able to grab them.

Party Starters

At the beginning of the party, play a tape of animal sounds as kids are arriving. Put out some easy animal jigsaw puzzles for kids to take apart and put together.

You Look Beastly!

These creative critters are masks to wear, or purely for display. If they're for wearing, use a craft knife on a protected surface to cut eye holes and slits for ribbon ties.

You need:
- White paper plates
- Construction paper in assorted colors
- Washable markers or crayons
- Glue sticks

Beforehand: Cut out shapes as follows from variously colored construction paper. For both animals, cut oval eyeballs and round pupils; also cut out red tongues. For elephants, cut out long trunks, big ears, and triangular tusks. For hippos, cut out semicircles for ears and rectangles for teeth. To make a mouth that opens and closes for the hippo design, fold one paper plate in half and stack on another; glue the lower halves of the plates together. Assemble an animal face of each kind so that children can follow an example.

At the party: When each guest arrives, have her choose an animal design and color the paper plates to match the animal's skin (or any color she thinks is right).

For the elephant, help the child mark eyes, then glue on a trunk, ears, and tusks. Curl each of these pieces forward by rolling them up and releasing them.

For the hippo, have the child glue on ears, teeth, eyes, and tongue, and draw on big nostrils.

Activities

Animal Rescue

Before the party, or while the kids are eating, hide plastic animal figures. Announce: "The animals have escaped from the zoo! Help us round them up." Give each child a strawberry basket to "cage" the critters they find. Afterwards, kids might set up a miniature zoo.

Feed the Seal
You need:
- ¾ yard of blue self-adhesive vinyl
- Foam board, 25" × 30"
- Large bucket
- 24 rubber or plastic fish

Beforehand: Make the seal bucket as follows.

1. Make a pattern of a seal large enough to fill the foam board, taping large pieces of paper together as necessary. Cut it out and use it as a pattern to cut out a seal from the blue vinyl.
2. Measure the height of the bucket, and adhere the seal to the board so that it will be centered right above the bucket.
3. Mark the words "Feed the Seal" on the board.

To play: Have kids stand at least 2 feet from the
bucket—farther for older kids. Let kids take
turns trying to toss fish into the bucket.

Who in the Zoo Are You?

Kids do great animal impressions. Warm them up by
asking, "Who can walk like an elephant? Who can bark
like a seal?" Hand out pictures of various animals: You
might use coloring book pages, magazine cutouts, animal lotto playing cards, or your own simple drawings.
Tell the kids not to let anyone see their animal. Each
child must act out her animal and the rest of the children
have to guess what it is.

Food

Zoo Bars

Cut brownies or cake into squares. Ice half of each with
frosting tinted blue, for the sky, the other half with icing
tinted green, for grass. Lay an animal cracker cookie
centered on top. Use chocolate decorator icing with a
fine tip to draw vertical cage "bars," or a simple fence. If
you'd like to make a fancy presentation, cover a large
platter with white paper, draw a pond in the middle, and
arrange the zoo bars around it. Put birthday candles in
the zoo bars.

Story Time

If I Ran the Zoo by by Dr. Seuss (Random
House). Rare and wonderful animals are assembled in a youngster's imagination.

Brown Bear, Brown Bear, What Do You See? by Eric Carle (Henry Holt). Tissue paper collages and simple, rhyming text engage readers in guessing which creature will appear next in the story. Kids will enjoy making predictions using the visual and verbal clues.

Party Favor

Draw black zebra stripes on white bags and fill them with any of the following: zoo animal rings, hanging monkeys plastic toys, animal stickers, and animal crackers.

Happy Half Birthday

Honor a fractional birthday with a full measure of fun. Perhaps your child's birthday falls at a less than optimum time—too close to Christmas or during a vacation when friends aren't around. Sometimes a family situation makes a celebration at the regular time inconvenient, or your child's preferred party activities are out of sync with the season of her birth. Why not throw a party six months later (or earlier)? Celebrate a half-birthday!

Invitation
Glue a white half-moon to dark blue paper and scatter star stickers around it. Announce that the party will begin on the half hour, of course!

Decorations
- Hang construction paper or craft-foam shapes so that they can turn in the breeze: semicircles, ½ fraction signs, half stars, half hearts.

Party Starters

Crazy Combos
You need:
- Magazine cutouts or drawings of various individual humans and animals, no larger than 5" × 7"

- Large index cards
- Scissors
- Glue stick

> **Beforehand:** Cut each figure out from its background and center it lengthwise on an index card, securing it with glue. Cut the figure in half horizontally.
>
> **At the party:** Let the kids put these pieces together in imaginative ways to create a character that is half one type, half another. The kids can glue the pieces to index cards or keep shuffling them.

Half-Another
Apply face makeup on one side of a child's face only.

Activities

Half-Tones
Fill bottles to various levels with water and let kids tap them with different utensils to create music.

Almost Follow-the-Leader
Tell kids to do half of what the leader does. For example, if the leader turns around in a circle, everyone turns only halfway. If she jumps twice, everyone jumps once. Give anyone with initiative a chance to be the leader.

Hoppy Half-a-Longs
Have a relay race in which kids hop on one foot.

Age Race

Mark a circular racecourse with a starting line and a halfway line. Have the kids run completely around the course as many times as the number of the birthday child's age and then run just to the halfway line. Have them call out the number each time they complete a lap, ending with a triumphant "and a half!" Be prepared for giddy confusion as they forget where to stop!

Half a Clue

Hide written clues that have been cut in half. Both pieces must be found and put together to find a prize. Or, hide pieces of a puzzle that kids must seek and piece.

Food

Half a Snack!

- Half a bagel, spread with peanut butter or cream cheese
- Apple halves, cored and rubbed with a lemon to prevent browning
- Cling peach halves

Half a Cake

Most supermarkets sell bundt cakes this way, but you could always bake a cake in two round pans, remove the layers, cut them in half, and stack the four semicircles with icing or jelly in between them. Put on the candles, making sure to break one of them in half.

Story Time

Birthday Happy, Contrary Mary by Anita Jeram (Candlewick). Contrary Mary isn't like other mice. Even at her birthday party, she sticks to her unique ways of doing things—eating Jell-O with a fork, playing on the floor while guests dance, even insisting that everyone wish her a "birthday happy."

Disney's The Little Mermaid by A. L. Singer (Disney Press). The most famous half person of all!

Party Favor

Draw a big "½" on a bag and fill it with a half pound of candy—perhaps candy fruit slices in semicircular shapes.

Plus one-half

Kids are often proud to announce, "I'm six and a half!" The party described on these pages suggests an alternative, not an addition, to the usual festivities at the yearly anniversary of a child's birth. No one who hosted a party six months in the past would want to throw another bash, or lead her child to expect any sort of gala repetition. However, there are lots of quiet and meaningful ways to commemorate a six-month milestone with your child:

- Mark the height of your child on a door frame or wall at his birthday and his half birthday.
- Take a half-day off from work and share it with your child in some special way.

- Buy a giant cookie and give your child half.
- Donate a Kennedy half-dollar to your child's piggy bank.
- Read half a story together and make up your own endings.
- Working with your child, go through toys or clothes he has outgrown and choose some to take to a charitable agency.

Island Event

Here's a fête to turn any day of the year into a summer vacation. This party has a mélange of flavors: Caribbean, Polynesian, Hawaiian, and Tahitian. Invite kids of any age, and get them in the "Don't Worry, Be Happy" mood with a few wearable accessories. Party stores carry hula skirts, or you can make your own with raffia or shredded paper. Tuck a flower behind each ear and everyone will feel the island spirit.

Invitation

If you know anyone going on an island vacation, ask them to bring you a bunch of scenic postcards. Or make postcards yourself: Go over 3" × 5" pieces of watercolor paper with watercolors, using horizontal strokes and enough water so that the colors run together and make a beautiful sunset. Cut some appropriate images from magazines and glue them to the pieces of watercolor paper. Write the party particulars and addressee on the back.

Decorations

- Cultivate "hibiscus flowers"! From red or pink crêpe paper, cut out 5"-diameter circles. Pinch the center, inserting a few artificial flower stamens. Make lots, then, using a yarn needle, thread onto string to make garlands.
- Strew seashells and coconuts along the center of the food table.

- Using large sheets of butcher paper, cut out curvy palm tree trunks. Fold 36"-long sheets of green crêpe paper lengthwise in half, and cut fringes, for palm fronds. Tape everything to a door or a wall.
- Hot-glue a scallop or clam shell to the base of each bulb on a string of Christmas lights. String them in houseplants, bushes, or wherever they add a festive touch.

Party Starters

Put out boxes or dishes of any of the items listed below, along with 1-yard lengths of colorful worsted-weight yarn and blunt tapestry or plastic yarn needles. Supply toddlers with shoelaces or licorice strings instead of yarn and needles. Let the kids string whatever they like onto their leis, and then tie the leis around each child's head or neck.

- Big wood beads
- Colorful, large plastic pony beads
- Penne or tube-shaped pasta, dyed with food coloring
- Inexpensive fabric flowers, cut from their garlands or stems
- Sections of pastel egg cartons, cut to simulate flowers
- Seashells gathered from the beach (use a dremel drill to add holes)
- 3" squares of brightly colored tissue paper, crushed into balls
- Flower shapes cut from colorful magazine pages (punch a hole in the center)

- 2"-diameter circles cut from craft foam (use scissors with a decorative edge)

Activities

Reggae and Calypso Band
Beforehand, prepare some instruments:

- Maracas: Throw some dried beans or rice in an empty food container and snap on the plastic lid. Hot-glue a dowel to the bottom for a handle. Paint each maraca with bright color stripes. Shake!

- Steel Drums: Hot-glue a series of small to large empty tin cans to a board. For drumsticks, metal and wood spoons will produce different effects. Tap!

- Coconut Ukulele: Drain a coconut and then crack or saw it in half. Hammer four brads or tacks at the top and bottom and stretch rubber bands of various widths between them. Strum!

- Guitar: Cut a big hole in the lid of a shoe box. For a neck, make a slit in one end of the box, and insert a ruler. Put the lid on the box and stretch rubber bands lengthwise around the box. For a bridge, place a pencil under the bands, on the side of the hole opposite the neck. Strum!

- Marimba or Xylophone: Lay a set of small wrenches across an egg carton, arranging them from smallest to largest and wedging the shanks between the compartments. Bang on them with butter knives. Bing, bong, boing, ting!

- Sandpaper Blocks: Buy or assemble pairs of sanding blocks. Rub them together. Scritch, scratch!

- Pipes: Fill various bottles with different amounts (and different colors!) of water. Set them in a row on a table. Blow across them, or tap them with a butter knife. Whooo!
- Bongo Drums: Use two empty oatmeal containers with plastic lids. On each, cut away the bottom; also cut out the center of the lid, leaving only a ring. For a skin, center a 10" square from a plastic bag over the top of each cylinder, secure with the lid ring, pulling the plastic taut. Join the two drums with masking tape or duct tape. Tap, tap with fingertips!

  At the party: Pass out the instruments. Play a little reggae music ("Reggae for Kids" [R.A.S.] is a wonderful tape!) while kids add their own rhythm and sound, a sort of instrumental karaoke. For each new song, have the kids switch instruments.

Limbo!
Obtain a 6-foot length of bamboo from an import or garden-supply store. Have some gentle reggae tunes running on a tape player. Ask older siblings to monitor the level of the pole and see how low, bending backwards at the knees, each child can go.

Hula Hoops
Have a contest to see how long the kids can keep a hoop going. Provide a bunch to compare, or clock individual times.

Luau

Volcano

Build up a mountain of chips, with a cup of mild salsa in the middle.

Beachfront Fruit

Lay a watermelon on its side and cut off the top. Scoop out the fruit and cut it into chunks. Carve waves along one side of the shell, and insert tiny paper parasols, for beach umbrellas, on the other side. Fill the shell with the watermelon chunks and pieces of other melons, pineapple, kiwi, banana, mango, plus grapes and a few maraschino cherries, both cut in half lengthwise.

Island Cake

Bake a banana cake mix in a 9" × 13" pan. Cool, then frost with vanilla or cream cheese frosting tinted with blue food coloring. Using a small spatula, swirl waves of frosting toward the center. To make a sandy island, form a 2"-deep strip of cardboard into a ring about 6" in diameter and place it lightly in the center of the cake; pulverize some sugar cookies, sprinkle the crumbs inside this ring, then remove it. To make palm trees, insert carrots into the island; top each with a canopy made by cutting a green pepper in half horizontally in a zigzag pattern (remove the seeds and use a dab of frosting to secure). Embellish the cake with gummy fish in the water and chocolate shell candies along the edge of the island—and don't forget the candles.

Polynesian Cocktails

Freeze cranberry-raspberry juice in ice cube trays until solid. Place 2 in each glass (use clear plastic); fill with pineapple juice. Dress up the cocktails with fruit chunks or slices skewered or slit to fit over the rim of the glass, and a palm-tree drink stirrer, a flexible or twirly straw, or a paper umbrella.

Story Time

Hawaii Is a Rainbow by Stephanie Feeney (University of Hawaii Press). Gorgeous photos teach colors while giving an idea of the variety of life.

Party Favor

Tie a bag with raffia and dangle a seashell from it. Inside, guests will be happy to find butterfly, parrot, or flower stickers or tattoos; plastic sunglasses; soap in the shape of a seashell or starfish; a bottle of bubbles; or a sailboat for the bathtub.

Ice Cream Social

What child could resist a sundae-making extravaganza? This old-fashioned event for all ages is a guaranteed hit: After all, who doesn't like ice cream? These days, sherbet, sorbet, gelato, frozen pudding, frozen custard, frozen yogurt, and Italian ice are variously and regionally hot! At RSVP time, when you become aware of any lactose-intolerant attendee, you'll know to plan on having some nondairy options available.

Invitation

Make a flyer for "Jody's Ice Cream Parlor." To begin, fold an 8½" × 11" piece of paper widthwise into thirds. Let the bottom two-thirds represent a storefront window: Outline a big ice cream cone; next to it write all the party particulars.

Photocopy the sheet for each invitation. To simulate an awning, cut scallops into the top edge. If your child is over 5, ask him to stripe the awning and fill in the ice cream cone graphic using pastel markers. Fold up the bottom third of the paper, then fold down the awning and secure it with tape. Write the address on the back.

Decorations

- Instead of one large dining table, set up several small tables with just two or three chairs each.
- Choose bright pastel party goods—streamers, tablecloth, paper and plastic tableware—in raspberry,

mint green, and lemon yellow. Helium balloons will add a festive touch.

- Letter a sign to say "Jody's Ice Cream Parlor" on clear plastic. Tape the sign in a window so that it reads backwards as if you're inside the store.
- Paint giant ice cream cones, parfaits, and sundaes on heavy paper; cut them out and tape them up all around the area.
- On a chalkboard, write "Menu" and draw in a few cones and sundaes. You'll fill in the selections later.

Party Starters

Scoop Challenges

- "How far can you walk balancing an ice cream cone on your head?" As each guest arrives, place an empty ice cream cone, upside down, on top of his head and point him down a course (hallway); place a piece of masking tape marked with his name on the floor to record the distance.
- "How many scoops can you fit on your ice cream cone?" Stage this outdoors or someplace easy to sweep up. Put out waffle cones (or paper ice cream cups, which are less likely to crumble) and an ice cream ball scoop (the kind with a releasing lever) and a bucket of "ice cream"—actually instant mashed potatoes or wet sand. Have the kids count as they fill their cones with scoops of mock ice cream. Be sure to have the kids throw away these cones afterwards!

Activities

Old-fashioned Games
Any of these will be a success: sack race, three-legged race, wheelbarrow race, and egg-on-a-spoon race—you could use maraschino cherries in place of eggs. Challenge older kids to carry the spoon handle in their mouths.

Menu

Name Your Sundae
If you wish, set this up as a buffet and either let the children spoon on their own toppings or enlist several teens or adults to fix custom sundaes. Set out bowls, several flavors of ice cream, and an array of toppings: fruit slices, sauces, sprinkles, cookie and candy bits, whipped cream in pressurized cans (kids will need some help with this), and maraschino cherries. For fun, use waffle cone bowls—everyone eats the contents of the bowl, then the bowl itself, so no disposable bowls are necessary.

PARENTS ALERT

Be sure to cut fruit into small chunks if there are toddlers at your party.

Encourage each child to concoct the sundae of her dreams, then ask her to give it a name so that you can record it on the chalkboard menu. In addition to the name, be sure to include a description of everyone's concoction. If the kids need a prompt, begin by naming your own sundae something like "Superior Sundae Chez Mom: coffee ice cream with chocolate chips, hot fudge, and raspberries." Outrageous names are fine, but assure shy or very young kids that simple ones like "Tommy's Treat" are just as delicious. After the party, type up the list. It will be a good souvenir for your child and would make a clever attachment to her thank-you notes.

Birthday-Cake Cones

The highlight of this menu is the custom sundae making, but if your child wants a cake so she can blow out the candles, here is a suggestion: Using a cake mix, prepare cake batter. Set flat-bottomed cake cones into the cupped sections of muffin pans. Pour the batter halfway into each cone. Bake in the oven for no longer than the time prescribed for cupcakes—check for doneness and remove the pans when a toothpick inserted into the cake comes out dry. Frost the cakes, insert a candle in each, and arrange on a platter. Once the candles are out, allow the kids to add decorations from the sundae-making buffet.

Story Time

Curious George Goes to an Ice Cream Shop by Margret Rey (Houghton Mifflin). The little monkey gets in and out of trouble, as usual.

The Banana Split from Outer Space by Catherine Siracusa (Hyperion Books). Stanley's ice cream business suffers until he meets an alien.

Ice Cream Bear by Jez Alborough (Candlewick Press). A bear falls asleep and dreams it's snowing ice cream!

Party Favor

Fill a plastic parfait dish with little sweets wrapped in colorful cellophane. Tie up the cellophane with cascades of curling ribbon.

"IT WORKED FOR ME"

"I always make up extra goody bags. Inevitably, one bag breaks, a big or little sister comes with mom to pick up her sibling, or somebody's cousin comes to town. Kids who couldn't make it to the party might surprise us by coming over later with a gift, and it's nice to be able to hand them a token as thanks."

Birthday Blizzard

There's snow time like winter for a party that's totally cool! Take advantage of all a snow-covered landscape has to offer. This is a good party for a crowd—adults and kids, family and friends. Responsible folk will look out for the littlest ones, taking any who look too damp and frosty inside. Have plenty of dry socks and extra mittens, hats, and scarves on hand for quick changes—you can only have fun if you're comfortably dressed!

Invitation

Cut a snowflake from copy paper. You know how: Fold a square into quarters, then diagonally in half. Or, if you want a six-sided snowflake, fold a circle in half, then into thirds. Cut little geometric shapes along the folds, and snip the open edges in a curve. Unfold and voilà! Glue it to black construction paper. Write the party specifics on the snowflake and photocopy. Ask guests to arrive dressed for the outdoors and to bring a change of clothing, in case various articles get wet. If you have access to a slope, suggest they bring sleds.

Decorations

- Let Mother Nature provide the outdoor decor. Add a "Birthday Lodge" sign, if you like.
- Enlist everyone's help cutting and hanging paper snowflakes indoors or on the porch.
- Decorate the windows with spray-snow motifs.

Party Starters

If children arrive dressed and equipped for sledding, why delay the fun? Adults can pull the kids on a flat surface and supervise downhill sledding.

Snowball Molding

Ask kids to mold a few balls in their hands and carry them on trash can lids to a place a few feet from the Snowy Peaks board, described below.

Favor the Birds

Beforehand: Set this up indoors or in a sheltered spot outside. For each child, wrap a pipe cleaner around a large pine cone and twist the ends together, making a hanging loop. Put out a cake of suet and plastic spoons or knives. Pour wild bird seed into a disposable aluminum roasting pan. Write each child's name on a wax paper sandwich bag so he'll be able to carry his treat home neatly. Provide packaged wipes for hand cleaning.

At the party: Let the kids coat the pine cones in suet, using the plastic utensils, and then roll the pine cones in the seed. Put each treat in a wax paper bag.

Activities

Snowy Peaks

Beforehand: To indicate a mountain range target, paint zigzags of various heights on a large sheet of plywood or masonite, and prop it securely

against a tree or fence. On the ground, make one
or two snow hollows to hold the snowball am-
munition.

At the party: Let kids use the snowballs they
molded for you to add some snow to those
peaks. The youngest kids should stand just 3 or
4 feet away, while adults with good throwing
arms may have to stand in the next town.

Snow Sculpture

Of course, you need good packing snow to sculpt a large
form from rolled balls of snow. But if you're in luck, ini-
tiate a group project. Ask the birthday child to choose
what sort of creature should be made—a big seated dog,
cat, or bunny rabbit is just as much fun and a little different from the standard snowman.

Snow Angels

If the snow is fairly powdery, or if you can schedule this
activity so that participants may change out of wet
clothes afterwards, this is a heavenly project. Have kids
lie down on their backs in the snow and wave their arms
and legs, keeping them straight. Have a strong person
help each child to get up so that the impressions won't
be disturbed.

The Blank Canvas

Kids become the artists! Give them squirt guns, plant
misters, and squeeze bottles filled with water that you've
tinted with food coloring. Line them up and set them to
work "painting" the snow—abstract masterpieces are
practically guaranteed.

Food

Cookout

Have a cookout in the snow! If you have lots of adults to share supervision, build a campfire so that everyone can get warm while you cook. Otherwise, get out the grill and make hamburgers, hot dogs, whatever your child's friends appreciate.

Cocoa au crème

Prepare hot cocoa and pour into large thermoses. Serve in insulated cups with a squirt of whipped cream or small marshmallows.

Igloo Cake

Prepare cake batter and bake in a large ovenproof bowl. Invert the cake onto a flat serving tray covered with freezer paper. To create an entranceway, place a cylindrical snack cake on its side adjacent to the domed cake. Frost everything with white icing. To suggest ice-block construction, press a grid into the frosting with a skewer. Add some snow people: For each, skewer three marshmallows on a toothpick. Use decorator icing with a writing tip to add features and to affix it to the paper-covered tray. Also affix flat candies in a curvy path up to the igloo entrance. If you're pine-ing for some landscaping, make fir trees, using a leaf tip or star tip to pipe green and white decorator icing over ice cream sugar cones.

Story Time

The Biggest Snowball Ever by John Rogan (Candlewick). When the kids decide to make "the biggest snowball ever," they get their wish, creating a monster snowball that threatens to roll over the town. This comical tale of trying to tame a runaway snowball will have kids rolling on the floor.

White Bear, Ice Bear by Joanne Ryder (Mulberry Books). A boy experiences life as a polar bear.

Party Favor

Decorate plain paper bags with rubber stamp snowflakes (ask your child to help if he's 4 or over) and write a guest's name on each. Insert a snow-block mold on which you've written the guest's name in permanent marker. Or, add some rock candy and a prism refractor or other optical toy.

"IT WORKED FOR ME"

"My little one picked out the stationery for the thank-you notes, signed her name following my brief words, and put stickers on the envelope flaps."

INDEX